Pastoral Crisis Intervention

D1706428

Pastoral Crisis Intervention

□□□

George S. Everly, Jr., PhD

The Johns Hopkins University Bloomberg School of Public Health Center for
Public Health Preparedness;
The Johns Hopkins University School of Medicine; and
Loyola College in Maryland

Pastoral Crisis Intervention

© 2007 George S. Everly, Jr.
Published by Chevron Publishing Corp.
5018 Dorsey Hall Drive, Suite 104
Ellicott City, MD 21042

Cover design by Peggy Johnson
Edited by Diane Gwin
Layout design by Peggy Johnson

Printed in the United States of America.
This book is printed on acid-free paper.

Library of Congress Card Catalog Number
Application in process

ISBN-10: 1-883581-18-4
ISBN-13: 978-1883581-18-3

CHEVRON
PUBLISHING CORPORATION

5018 Dorsey Hall Drive, Suite 104
Ellicott City, MD 21042 USA
Telephone: (410) 740-0065
Fax: (410) 740-9213
office@chevronpublishing.com

Dedication

To my children, Marideth, George, and Andi

"A Father's Prayer"

Each night, I pray to God that I may have the wisdom, the strength, and the compassion to be all that my children need in a father. I pray that I can show unconditional love and support without over indulgence in worldly goods, nor setting inappropriate expectations for the nature of the world in which they will live.
And when I am gone from this world, I hope to be judged not by how much I made, but by how much I gave;
Not by how many names I dropped, but by how many people hear my name and think fondly of me;
I hope my children will say of me he was wise, he was silly, with all of his flaws he was still a good man, he was there for us. He taught us the value of honesty, fidelity, of family and of friends, but above all else, he loved us, he was there when we needed him…
he will be with us always.

Acknowledgements

My interest in pastoral crisis intervention (PCI) reaches back 40 years, but without the assistance of the following individuals, my conceptualization of PCI, and of course this book, would never have been realized. I wish to sincerely thank and acknowledge the debt owed to the following individuals: Rev. Charles Bolin (a pioneer in non-traditional institutional pastoral crisis intervention), Rev. Rob Dewey (whose community-based crisis chaplaincy program represents a prime exemplar of pastoral crisis intervention in programmatic form worthy of note and replication), Rev. George Grimm, Rev. Glenn Calkins, and Rev. Ed Stauffer, (three true pioneers who have taught me much), Rev. Dr. Warren Ebinger and Mary Ebinger, (both of whom have provided religious support and pastoral crisis intervention to our family in times of need), Dr. Deborah Haskins (a respected colleague at Loyola College in Maryland with whom I have enjoyed many stimulating conversations on these matters), Rev. Dr. Thomas Hilt, Rev. Thomas Webb (who has intellectually extended the original pastoral crisis intervention model), and to Dr. James Reese and his wife Sandy, as well as Cherie Castellano and her husband Mark, whose personal and spiritual support have been most appreciated.

I would also like to thank Dr. Lee McCabe at the Johns Hopkins School of Medicine and Dr. Michael Kaminsky, also at the Johns Hopkins School of Medicine. Dr. McCabe has taken the original pastoral crisis intervention concept, as well as practice, and significantly expanded it into a model for application to specific spiritual and religious communities. Dr. Kaminsky has provided unwavering support, and through his model of Resistance, Resiliency, and Recovery, provided a firm platform for better understanding all crisis and disaster mental health interventions. Doctors McCabe and Kaminsky are both gentlemen and scholars, but most importantly I am privileged to call them friends.

I am also grateful to another Hopkins colleague, Dr. Jon Links, Professor and Director of the Johns Hopkins Center for Public Health Preparedness. One of the nation's leading authorities on "dirty bombs" and radiologic weapons of mass destruction, the support of Dr. Links has been invaluable in expanding the field of disaster mental health. Similarly, without his friendship and support the Center's model of psychological first aid would never have been developed.

Lastly, I must thank Dr. Steve Sobelman and Sloane Brown, as well as Dr. Douglas Strouse and Dr. Cindy Parker. Words cannot express the debt owed or the gratitude felt.

Blessed is he who is surrounded by those of a good heart and an unwavering supportive presence…I am truly blessed.

□□□

Disclaimer

The material in this text is provided as a general overview and reference only. It is not intended to be a clinical prescription, nor treatment manual. Nor is the material in this text designed to be used by anyone other than those already trained to do so.

About the Author

□□□

George S. Everly, Jr., PhD, ABPP coined the term "pastoral crisis intervention" in a seminal paper published in the year 2000. He has subsequently published and conducted numerous training programs on the topic. For nine years, he specialized in the treatment of stress and stress-related disorders, having been Chief Psychologist and Director of Behavioral Medicine at the Johns Hopkins Homewood Hospital Center much of that time. He later studied the most severe form of human stress…posttraumatic stress disorder (PTSD). His observations in 20 countries on six continents serve as an additional backdrop for the material in this volume. In his role as a mental health advisor in the wake of mass disasters such as the Oklahoma City bombing, Hurricane Andrew, Hurricane Katrina, the devastation of Kuwait after the Iraqi invasion, the terrorist attacks of 9/11, and SARS, he has gained a truly unique perspective on how human beings react in highly stressful situations. More importantly, however, he is uniquely qualified to offer insight into the nature of human resiliency in the wake of extreme adversity.

Dr. Everly currently serves on the faculties of The Johns Hopkins Center for Public Health Preparedness, The Johns Hopkins University Bloomberg School of Public Health, The Johns Hopkins University School of Medicine, and Loyola College in Maryland. In addition, he lectures frequently at the Federal Emergency Management Agency, the FBI National Academy, and has served on the U.S. Centers for Disease Control Mental Health Exemplars Committee. He is an advisor to the Hospital Authority of Hong Kong. He was formerly Senior Research Advisor, Social Development Office, Office of His Highness, the Amir of Kuwait, State of Kuwait. Prior to these appointments, Dr. Everly was a Harvard Scholar, Visiting in Psychology, Harvard University; a Visiting Lecturer in Medicine, Harvard Medical School; and, Chief Psychologist and Director of Behavioral Medicine for the Johns Hopkins' Homewood Hospital Center.

Dr. Everly is a Fellow of the American Institute of Stress, has been awarded the Fellow's Medal of the Academy of Psychosomatic Medicine and the Professor's Medal of the Universidad de Weiner (Peru). He is the author, co-author, or editor of 15 textbooks and more than 100 professional papers. Among his texts are *Mental Health Aspects of Disasters: Public Health Preparedness and Response* (Johns Hopkins, 2005), Psychological Counterterrorism and World War IV (Chevron, 2005), *Personality Guided*

Therapy of Posttraumatic Stress Disorder (APA, 2004), *Critical Incident Stress Management*, 2nd Edition (Chevron, 1999), *Psychotraumatology* (Plenum, 1995), *A Clinical Guide to the Treatment of the Human Stress Response*, 2nd Edition (Plenum, 2002), *Controlling Stress and Tension*, 7th Edition (Allyn Bacon, 2005), and *Personality and Its Disorders*, with Theodore Millon (Wiley, 1985).

Dr. Everly has won numerous awards, receiving the Certificate of Honor from the Baltimore Police Department, the Honor Award from the American Red Cross, the Leadership Award from the American Red Cross, and the Maryland Psychological Association's Award for Scientific Contributions to Psychology. Dr. Everly was the recipient of the University of Maryland's College of Health and Human Performance's 50th Anniversary Outstanding Alumni Award and was recognized as a "Pioneer in Clinical Traumatology" by the Traumatology Institute of the Florida State University. He served as the Mental Health Chairperson for the Central Maryland Chapter of the American Red Cross, where he was co-founder of the disaster mental health network. In addition, he assisted in the development of the State of Maryland Disaster Mental Health Corps and Maryland's Disaster Spiritual Care Corps. Dr. Everly was the 39th president of the Maryland Psychological Association. He has given invited lectures in 22 countries on 6 continents. His works have been translated into Russian, Arabic, Swedish, Polish, Portuguese, Japanese, Chinese, German, Korean, and Spanish. His biography appears in Who's Who in America and Who's Who in the World.

Table of Contents

Chapter One

A Time of Need

We have entered a new millennium. We do so with great expectations of exciting things to come. New discoveries and great improvements in life will surely be coupled with new challenges, even traumas.

□□□

A Changing World

Within recent years, we have witnessed a series of domestic and global changes that will surely alter expectations of the future and potentially serve to challenge our sense of prosperity and well-being. Consider that within recent years we have experienced:

1. the collapse of the Soviet Empire and resultant political and financial instability throughout most of Eastern Europe;

2. the rise of China as a major economic and military power;

3. a reorganization of the American healthcare system wherein the quality of healthcare is seen by many as having been sacrificed for economy;

4. the emergence of the most vitriolic political schism in recent memory;

5. the meteoric rise and catastrophic collapse of the "high tech" industrial and telecommunications sectors leaving a wake of financial ruin;

6. a scandal within the accounting industry that has cast doubt upon the integrity and vitality of the icons of American capitalism, especially the stock market;

7. the destruction of the World Trade Center in New York City;

8. the attack on the Pentagon with the subsequent release of anthrax within the U.S. Postal System;

9. the advent of the war against terrorism; "We are in a war that will set the course for a new century." Winning the war against terrorism is the "calling of our generation." according to President George W. Bush on 09/11/06;

10. the invasion of Afghanistan, on-going military confrontations in Iraq;

11. the potential for nuclear conflict between India and Pakistan;

12. the rise of potential nuclear arsenals in North Korea and Iran;

13. an immigration crisis in which a flood of illegal immigrants is changing the structure and function of American culture;

14. the potential for the use of stem cells to re-grow damaged human organs; and

15. the cloning of mammalian life forms.

For many, the aforementioned challenges not only have economic and social ramifications, they have psychological, spiritual, and even religious implications, as well.

Mental Health Consequences

What might be the mental health consequences of an epidemic of change and turmoil? An overarching concept that seems applicable is that of "crisis." A crisis may be thought of as a response to an event, or critical incident, wherein one's usual coping mechanisms have failed and there is evidence of clinically significant distress or dysfunction (Everly & Mitchell, 1999, adapted from Caplan, 1961, 1964).

What is the magnitude of risk for experiencing a significant critical incident or trauma that might yield a crisis or some otherwise significantly adverse impact upon one's mental and /or spiritual health? What are the mental health consequences of such exposure?

- Evidence suggests that more than 60% of adults in the United States will be exposed to a traumatic event during their lifetime (Breslau, et at., 1998).

- The rate of trauma exposure for children and adolescents has been estimated to be about 40% (see Ford, Ruzek, and Niles, 1996).

- The conditional risk of developing posttraumatic stress disorder (PTSD) was found to be 13% for females and 6% for males in a general community sample (Breslau, et al., 1998).

- Suicide rates have been seen to increase 62% in the first year after an earthquake, increase 31% in the first two years after a hurricane, and increase by almost 14% four years after a flood (Krug, et at., 1998).

- Each year, approximately one million persons become victims of violent crime at work (Bachman, 1994).

- The prevalence of PTSD was found to be 13% in a sample of suburban law enforcement officers (Robinson, Sigman, and Wilson, 1997).

- Law enforcement officers are 8.6 times more likely to die from suicide than from homicide and are 3.1 times more likely to die from suicide than from accidental circumstances (Violanti, 1996).

- The prevalence of posttraumatic stress disorder ranged from 15% to 31% for samples of urban firefighters, based on a traumatic exposure prevalence ranging from 85% to 91% (Beaton, Murphy, and Corneil, 1996).

- Symptoms of distress and PTSD are correlated with exposure to traumatic stressors (Weiss et al., 1995; Corneil, 1993; Wee, et al., 1999).

- According to a national poll conducted by the American Red Cross (ARC, 2001) from October 5 to 8, 2001, 20% of the American public reported significant psychological symptoms related to the terrorist attacks of 2001.

- In the Fall of 1991, what has been called the deadliest shooting in U.S. history occurred in Kileen, Texas (North et al., 1994). North and her colleagues (North et al., 2002) followed the longitudinal course of this event from a psychiatric perspective. The rates of PTSD, major depression, and panic at the 6-8 week baseline for a sample of 136 were 28.8%, 10.3%, and 2.3%, respectively. At the one year follow-up (n=124), those rates were 17.7%, 4.9%, and 2.4%, respectively. There were no cases of delayed onset PTSD. Overall recovery from PTSD at the 3 year assessment was about 50%.

- Subsequent to the September 11, 2001, terrorist attacks on the World Trade Center, during the period from October 11 through December, 2001, the CDC Behavioral Risk Factor Surveillance System (BRFSS) initiative sampled 3,512 adult residents of Connecticut, New Jersey, and New York via a random digit dialed telephonic survey. The "results of the survey suggest a widespread psychological and emotional impact in all segments of the three states' populations" (CDC, 2002, p.784) Seventy-five percent of respondents reported having problems attributed to the attacks: 48% of respondents reported that they experienced anger after the attacks, 37.5% reported worry, 23.9 reported nervousness, and 14.2% reported sleep disturbance. About 12% of respondents reported receiving help, but the majority of the help received was from family members and friends.

- Galea, Ahern, et al. (2002) assessed the prevalence of acute posttraumatic stress disorder (PTSD) and depression among residents of Manhattan five to eight weeks after the terrorist attacks of September 11. Among those interviewed, 7.5% reported symptoms consistent with a diagnosis of current PTSD related to the attacks and 9.7% reported symptoms consistent with depression occurring within the previous 30 days. Among respondents who lived closer to Ground Zero, south of Canal, the prevalence of PTSD was 20%.

- Stein, et al. (2004) conducted a longitudinal study of the psychological consequences of the September 11 terrorist attacks. The investigation yielded a 71% response rate with the following findings:

  16% of adults reported 1 or more symptoms of significant distress. Of that 16%...

  65% reported accomplishing less at work (33% overall);

  75% turned to prayer, or spirituality (58% overall); while

  43% reported using alcohol or other chemicals to reduce distress (17% overall).

- Subsequent to another terrorist attack on American soil, North, et al. (1999) assessed the prevalence of psychiatric disorders amongst a cohort of 255 survivors of the Oklahoma City bombing at 6 months post event. Results indicated that 45% of the subjects possessed a psychiatric disorder. The authors report the onset of symptoms was rapid (76% reporting same day onset).

Contributing Factors?

We observe these outcomes against a backdrop of what some have considered an epidemic of moral decay in American society. In 1967, Thomas Harris wrote a book entitled *I'm OK – You're OK*. Based upon the work of Eric Berne, it became the mantra of the 1960s and 1970s. While the book described a highly useful Transactional Analysis approach to understanding human behavior, it perhaps inadvertently did much more. The title itself served as the mantra that would serve to blur the distinction between right and wrong while serving to justify virtually all forms of human behavior as acceptable variations. Rather than identifiable extremes on a continuum of human behavior, the difference between right and wrong became blurred by a gray middle ground of compromise wherein we became afraid to even suggest that certain behaviors were unacceptable. Thomas Paine stated in *Common Sense* that "A long habit of not thinking a thing wrong gives it a superficial appearance of being right." Have we risked such an outcome in the name of "political correctness?" Have we endorsed divorce and the dissolution of the family by choosing not to proclaim the often realized adverse effects upon children and even the community. Have we inadvertently endorsed the notion that maintaining a healthy financial bottom line supersedes maintaining moral integrity and honesty? Can we really say that there is a right and a wrong or is moral relativism not only politically correct but socially syntonic? Perhaps there was some validity to that which Oscar Wilde once noted, "Morality, like art, means drawing a line someplace."

The "anything goes" era of the 1970s and 1980s spawned a plague of impulsiveness, insincerity, and irresponsibility - worse yet, moral relativism and a moral duplicity. As Bertrand Russell observed, "We have, in fact, two kinds of morality side by side: one which we preach but do not practice, and another which we practice but seldom preach."

We learned a series of platitudes by which we were to live that have come back to haunt us personally and even as a society. We were told, for example:

1. The end DOES justify the means.
2. If it feels good, do it!
3. Worry about it later.
4. Do unto others before they do unto you.
5. He/she who dies with the most "toys" wins.
6. Winning is not everything, it's the only thing.
7. Morality is relative.
8. We should not judge another's behavior.
9. We are not really responsible for our actions.
10. "The devil made me do it!" (a la comedian Flip Wilson)
11. The "ultimate" marriage vows for the 1970s: "We take one another as husband and wife for as long as we shall love."

We are now reaping the harvest that was sown then.
1. For every two marriages that occurred in the 1990s, there was one divorce.
2. The Enron scandal.
3. The collapse of the technology sector in the late 1990s contributed to by analysts inflating prognostications.
4. The WorldCom scandal.
5. The rise of a music genre that promotes sex, violence, and the dehumanization of women.

A Clash of Values

There appear to exist two diametrically opposed views, or values systems, that guide current behavior:

1. A perspective that values the PROCESS of our actions.

2. A perspective that values the OUTCOME of our actions.

We, as a society, remain consumed with achieving the things we want in life (outcome), without considering how we obtain them (process) and the "ripple effect" upon others created by our actions.

To value primarily the outcome achieved in life is an inherently flawed approach to prosocial living, for it neglects the impact of our actions upon others in lieu of the desired personal outcome ("The end justifies the means."). From a community perspective, it is asocial at best, antisocial at worst.

To address the self-centeredness of an outcome-driven approach to life and its adverse impact upon the community, an overarching mechanism of coherency is needed: A unifying construct such as faith, spirituality, religious belief, may serve such a purpose while also serving as a solid foundation upon which stress resistance and resiliency in the wake of s and traumatic events may be built.

Spirituality and Religion Defined

Psychologists have often considered spirituality and religion as one in the same (Zinnbauer & Pargament, 2005). This is an over-simplification and is indeed inaccurate.

Building on the definitions compiled by Zinnbauer and Pargament (2005), spirituality may be thought of as a subjective experience with relationship to or faith in some transcendent, sacred, or divine presence that usually serves to provide a sense of coherency to one's understanding of existence. Religion, on the other hand, may be thought of as a system of specific scripture or doctrine-specific beliefs, practices, and rituals relating the human presence to a divine presence as well as the practice of worship toward that divine presence.

Spiritual and Religious Implications

As we continue the search for an integrating model of coherency, we now consider the effects of faith, spirituality, and religion. We begin with the oft cited statistic that 97% of Americans believe in God and 90% pray. Further, more people believe in organized religion than any other organized social institution. A *USA Today-Gallup* poll sampled 1,037 American adults in late 1999. They found that: 30% described themselves as "spiritual," while 54% of respondents said they were religious. In a national survey conducted by the American Red Cross from October 5 – 8, 2001 (ARC, 2001), 59% of respondents said they would be likely or very likely to seek assistance from a spiritual counselor, this in comparison to seeking help from physicians (45%) or mental health professionals (40%).

Religious beliefs may be the single best predictor of abstinence from alcohol and drug abuse, as well as abstinence from premarital and extra-marital sexual activity (Spilka, et al., 2003). Following the terrorism of September 11, 2001, surveys reported an increase in church attendance ranging from 6% to 24%, but that such attendance was reduced to pre-September levels by the end of the year (Spilka, et al., 2003). These findings suggest that religion may serve to foster attitudes and behaviors that are pro-social and that foster community health. Further, they suggest that religion may be used as an acute stress management/coping intervention.

The notion that spirituality and religion may be used to cope with extreme stress is not new. Indeed, the old saying, "There are no atheists in a fox-hole" speaks to the idea that, when confronted with extreme adversity, people often look to a higher power for understanding, if not protection.

In his book *Lifesigns*, Heni Nouwen (1986) explains that fear blocks the achievement of intimacy, fecundity, and complete joy. He argues that fear may be overcome using religious belief.

But what of the whole notion of believing in God, to whom one looks in adversity? "Pascal's Wager" is the name given to a famous argument for believing in God. Pascal (1623 – 1662) was a French mathematician, physicist, and religious philosopher. In his *Pensées*, Pascal presents a "wager" for those who are skeptical about the existence of God. Pascal uses an analytical approach to the question. He notes, "God is, or He is not. But to which side shall we incline? Reason can decide nothing here…A game is being played at the extremity of this infinite distance where heads or tails will turn up...Which will you choose then? …Let us weigh the gain and the loss in wagering that God is. Let us estimate these two chances. If you gain, you gain all; if you lose, you lose nothing. Wager, then, without hesitation that He is."

Timothy Johnson's *Finding God in the Questions* (Johnson, 2004) may be a more modern version of Pascal's *Pensées*. In Johnson's "personal journey," he presents a compelling case for the existence of God, but rather than using Pascal's analytic approach, or some spiritual or religious doctrine, he presents a gentle yet persuasive rhetoric based on personal doubt, experience, and exploration. In his treatise on "final judgment," Johnson addresses the dogma of some strict orthodoxies by noting that, in the Christian Bible's presentation of the parable of final judgment according to Matthew, there is no mention of "correct thinking," no mention of correct political or social positions, no mention of time spent in traditional religious worship, and no mention of the acquisition of power, fame, or wealth.

Pastoral Resources

The spiritually-based or religion-based communities with their pastorally-oriented resources represent a large and often untapped resource in times of crisis and . They possess an aggregation of characteristics that make them uniquely valuable amidst the turmoil of a psychological crisis or simply as an infrastructure upon which a community may flourish. In critical incidents, such as terrorism, mass s, violence, the loss of loved ones, and any events wherein human actions result in injury, destruction, and/or death, the pastoral community may possess especially powerful restorative attributes. Unfortunately, heretofore, there have existed few generally recognized and accepted ways in which the healing factors inherent in pastoral care have been functionally integrated with the well-formulated principles of crisis intervention and mental health response (Verhoff, Kuhlka, and Couvan, 1981; Koenig, 2006). This book represents an effort to elucidate how the principles of pastoral care may be functionally integrated with those of crisis intervention and mental health. The amalgam shall hereafter be referred to as "pastoral crisis intervention" and is defined in this book.

□□□

Chapter Two

"Pastoral Crisis Intervention"

The term pastoral crisis intervention (Everly, 2000) is offered as a term that represents the functional integration of psychological crisis intervention with pastoral care. This chapter will examine the widely used definitions of both domains and will further seek to elucidate the foundations of functional integration.

☐☐☐

Crisis Intervention

Crisis intervention is best understood in the context of the term *crisis*. A *crisis* may be thought of as an acute *response* to an event wherein homeostasis is disrupted, one's usual coping mechanisms have failed, and there is evidence of significant distress or functional impairment (Everly & Mitchell, 1999, adapted from Caplan, 1961, 1964). The stressor event that precedes the crisis response is commonly referred to as the *critical incident*. The term *crisis intervention* refers to the provision of an acute helping process so as to progressively achieve 1) a stabilization of symptoms of distress, 2) mitigation of symptoms, and 3) restoration of adaptive, independent functioning, if possible, or facilitation of access to further support (Everly & Mitchell, 1999; Flannery & Everly, 2000).

In the formative years of crisis intervention, Rapoport (1965) noted, "A little help, rationally directed and purposely focused at a strategic time, is more effective than extensive help given at a period of less emotional accessibility" (p. 30). Later, Swanson and Carbon (1989) writing for the American Psychiatric Association Task Force Report on the Treatment of Psychiatric Disorders stated, "Crisis intervention is a proven approach to helping in the pain of an emotional crisis" (p. 2520).

The aforementioned assertions were made not based upon case study and field empiricism alone but also upon well-controlled clinical investigations. Let us briefly review the early foundations of crisis intervention and thus pastoral crisis intervention.

Langsley, Machotka, and Flomenhaft (1971) used random assignment (RCT) of 300 patients to inpatient treatment vs. family crisis intervention. Results indicated crisis intervention was superior to inpatient treatment for preventing subsequent psychiatric hospitalizations. Decker and Stubblebine (1972) followed 540 psychiatric patients for 2½ years subsequent to an initial psychiatric hospitalization. Traditional follow-up treatment was compared to crisis intervention services. Results supported the superiority of the crisis intervention services in preventing subsequent hospitalizations.

Bunn and Clarke (1979), in a randomized controlled design with 30 individuals who had accompanied relatives to the hospital after a serious injury, found 20 minutes of supportive crisis counseling superior to no intervention in reducing anxiety.

Bordow and Porritt (1979) employed a three group RCT of individual crisis intervention with hospitalized motor vehicle accident victims. Results were indicative of a dose response relationship between intervention level and the reduction of reported distress.

When crisis intervention principles and practices were applied to victims of bank robberies, the crisis interventions were found to be effective in reducing distress (Campfield & Hills, 2001; Richards, 2001). In military applications, Solomon and Benbenishty (1986) found the core crisis intervention principles of "proximity, immediacy, and expectancy" to be effective in response to combat; this is consistent with the seminal observations of Salmon (1919) and Artiss (1963). Deahl et al. (2000) found small group crisis intervention to be effective in reducing alcohol use in military personnel after returning from peace-keeping activities in a war zone. Most important, however, are the implications of a 20-year longitudinal study by Solomon and colleagues (Solomon, et al., 2005). The study evaluated the long-term effectiveness of frontline treatment provided to combat stress reaction casualties. Using a longitudinal quasi-experimental design, combat stress reaction casualties of the 1982 Lebanon War who received frontline treatment (N=79), were compared to comparable combat stress reaction casualties who did not receive frontline treatment (N=156), and other soldiers who did not experience combat stress reaction (N=194). Twenty years after the war, traumatized soldiers who received frontline crisis intervention, following the core principles of proximity, immediacy, expectancy, had lower rates of posttraumatic and psychiatric symptoms and reported better social functioning than similarly exposed soldiers who did not receive frontline intervention. The cumulative effect of the core crisis principles was documented in that the more principles applied, the stronger the effect. The authors conclude, "Frontline treatment is associated with improved outcomes even two decades after its application. This treatment may also be effective for nonmilitary precursors of posttraumatic stress disorder" (p. 2309).

Flannery (2001; Flannery, Hanson, Penk, Flannery, & Gallagher, 1995) pioneered the development of a multi-component critical incident stress management program referred to as the Assaulted Staff Action Program (ASAP). The ASAP program was chosen as one of the 10 best programs in 1996 by the American Psychiatric Association. A 10-year review of ASAP practice revealed ASAP to be clinically effective (Flannery, 2001). In a follow-up investigation, Flannery, Rego, Farley & Walker (in press) reported on a fifteen-year study of a CISM-oriented crisis intervention procedure to attend to the aftermath of workplace violence. The sample consisted of 1,071 male and 1,049 female inpatient and community mental health facilities staff victims of patient assaults in the Massachusetts Department of Mental Health's seven inpatient state hospitals, five state community mental health centers, one state homeless shelter program, two vendor-operated sets of community residences, and one private general hospital that accepted DMH patients. The crisis intervention procedures were associated with sharp declines in disruptions in the three health domains and the three symptom clusters. The findings demonstrate significant recovery and functioning within a ten-day period associated with the CISM intervention.

In the wake of a terrorist mass disaster, Boscarino, et al., (2005) conducted a random sample of 1,681 New York adults interviewed by telephone at 1 year and 2 years after September 11. Results indicate that crisis interventions, referred to as Critical Incident Stress Management (CISM), had a beneficial impact across a variety of outcomes, including reduced risks for binge drinking, alcohol dependence, PTSD symptoms, major depression, somatization, anxiety, and global impairment, compared with individuals who did not receive these interventions. In a follow-up analysis (Boscarino, et al., 2006), found that 1 to 3 sessions of brief crisis intervention were useful in reducing various forms of distress from mass disasters.

Stapleton and colleagues (in press) conducted a meta-analysis of 11 studies of crisis intervention with medical and surgical patients. The analysis included 2124 subjects. Stapleton et al., found crisis intervention to be generally effective overall (Cohen's $d = .44$), with specific mitigating effects on anxiety (.52), depression (.24), and posttraumatic stress (.57).

Finally, Everly et al. (in press) employed a systematic statistical review of experimental and quasi-experimental research on workplace-based crisis intervention programs. Nine studies were identified that met inclusion criteria for further analysis. Results suggest that the workplace can be a useful platform from which to provide crisis intervention programs (overall effectiveness measured in the Cohen's d statistic (expressed in standard deviations) = 1.53; d = .60 with assaults removed from the analysis). More specifically, evidence was found that crisis intervention programs could reduce specific undesirable factors in the workplace:

Posttraumatic distress:	mean effect size: .65
Assaults:	mean effect size: 3.68
Alcohol use:	mean effect size: .83

Depression:	.81
Anxiety:	.98
Global impairment:	mean effect size: .166

Pastoral Intervention

As defined herein, pastoral care may be seen as the function of providing a spiritual, religious, or faith oriented leadership. Pastoral care is typically provided by someone (often ordained, but not always) who has been commissioned or otherwise selected by a faith-oriented group, or other organization, to provide interpersonal support, assistance in religious education, worship, sacraments, community organization, ethical-religious decision-making, and related activities of spiritual support. From a more formal perspective, pastoral care is commonly provided by congregation-based clergy (and sometimes formally trained laity), chaplains, pastoral counselors, and clinical pastoral educators, while recognizing that these terms and functions are not mutually exclusive.

The opportunity for pastoral care interventions was formalized in the military on July 29, 1775, by an act of the Continental Congress. At that time, the Congress allowed for the creation of an organized military chaplaincy. The opportunity for pastoral care, of course, existed prior to that informally at any time a member of the "flock" would seek guidance or support from anyone held to be in a position of pastoral leadership.

Pastoral Counseling

One specialized form of pastoral care that has emerged is pastoral counseling. The process of pastoral counseling, in the generic sense, may be thought of as the utilization of psychological, spiritual, and theological resources to aid persons in psychological and/or spiritual distress (Clinebell, 1966; Hunter, 1990). Pastoral counseling is an approach to the therapeutic process, wherein theology and spirituality are integrated with the principles of psychology and behavioral science to help individuals, couples, families, groups, and institutions achieve mental health and promote wellness at all levels. Those who seek pastoral counseling typically feel that there is added value in a pastoral approach to healing over and above traditional counseling and psychotherapeutic practices. They come seeking counseling for personal, relationship, family, and even work-related concerns. Pastoral counselors may use traditional psychodiagnostic techniques, spiritually-based assessments, and traditional psychotherapeutic and behavioral therapy processes, in addition to spiritual and even religiously-based interventions.

The clinical pastoral education movement, beginning in the 1920s with the pioneering efforts of Richard Cabot and others, served as somewhat of a foundation for the outgrowth of the pastoral counseling emergence. During World War II, the function of pastoral counseling emerged as an important element of the services provided by military chaplains (Barry, 2003). Post WWII, the recognition of the need to provide chaplains with formalized training in counseling led to chaplains being sent to Catholic University and the Menninger Clinic in pursuit of such training (Barry, 2003).

In 1963, the American Association of Pastoral Counselors was formed. Thus, the integration of psychological principles and practices with pastoral care appears to be currently manifest in two formalized movements: pastoral counseling and clinical pastoral education.

Pastoral Crisis Intervention

It seems clear that anyone who serves the function of providing pastoral care will be confronted with the challenge of an acute psychological and/or spiritual crisis. Whether in a house of worship, a hospital, a nursing home, at the scene of an accident or disaster, a funeral home or gravesite, a battlefield, or even in a formalized counseling office setting, the manifestations of a human being in a state of crisis can be in evidence. The crises may manifest themselves in concrete and tangible concerns regarding safety, security, and general welfare, or they may manifest themselves in less tangible concerns regarding self-identity, affiliative crises, existential, spiritual, or even theological or theodilitic crises (a crisis of faith). But, contrary to some commonly held pastoral perspectives, not all crises are spiritually or theologically based (Sinclair, 1993). For those who rise to meet such challenges, a solid grounding in theology, spirituality, and pastoral care is only the beginning. Also requisite will be skills in psychological triaging, basic crisis intervention, and finally, a familiarity with other supportive resources, including psychological, psychiatric, and even other pastoral resources.

This then is the practice of *pastoral crisis intervention*. Simply stated, *pastoral crisis intervention is the functional integration of any and all religious, spiritual, faith-based, and pastoral resources with the assessment and intervention technologies germane to the practice of crisis intervention and disaster mental health.* Clearly, as is evident from the definition afforded earlier, crisis intervention is not the same as counseling and psychotherapy (Everly, 1999). Some psychotherapeutic tactics would even be contraindicated in crisis intervention due, in part, to the highly focused and time-limited nature of crisis intervention. Similarly, pastoral crisis intervention is not the same as pastoral counseling or pastoral psychotherapy. Thus, by way of summarial parallelism, as crisis intervention is to counseling and psychotherapy, so pastoral crisis intervention is to pastoral counseling and pastoral psychotherapy.

Webb (2004) has contributed the following notion of pastoral crisis intervention. "Shock waves from a traumatic event impact the entire individual and affect one's relationships horizontally with family, friends, and co-workers and vertically with God. Individuals can exhibit symptoms of traumatic stress in any or all of the five major domains: physical, cognitive, emotional, behavioral and spiritual. For this reason, [pastoral] crisis intervention combines the identity and skills from the spectrum of religious, spiritual, and pastoral resources with the assessment and intervention strategies pertinent to the practice of emergency mental health (Everly, 2000b). The "value added" of pastoral crisis intervention stems from hope-giving pastoral care and/or religious tradition and ritual resting upon a foundation of communication skills, differential recognition of patterns of acute stress, and traditional mechanisms of crisis intervention, such as early intervention, cathartic ventilation, social support, problem-solving, and cognitive reinterpretation (Everly, 2000b)" (Webb, 2004, p. 217).

Mechanisms of Action

The mechanisms of action which support pastoral crisis intervention include all of the same mechanisms which support non-pastoral crisis intervention, such as education, reassurance, social support, problem-solving, cathartic ventilation, and cognitive reinterpretation (Everly & Mitchell, 1999). In addition, the pastoral crisis interventionist benefits from the ability to use, where appropriate, scriptural education, insight, and reinterpretation (Brende, 1991), individual and conjoint prayer, a belief in the power of intercessory prayer, a unifying and explanatory spiritual worldview that may serve to bring order to otherwise incomprehensible events, the utility of ventilative confession, a faith-based social support system, the use of rituals and sacraments, and in some religions, such as Christianity, the notion of divine forgiveness and even a life after death. All of these factors may make unique contributions to the reduction of manifest levels of distress (Everly & Lating, 2002). Finally, the pastoral crisis interventionist may also prosper from a truly unique ethos (the perspective of pontifical, theological, or divine credibility), as well as the implicit belief in uniquely confidential/privileged communication exchange.

The two intervention processes closest to the extant definition of pastoral crisis intervention would appear to be crisis ministry and crisis chaplaincy. As commonly defined, crisis ministry has as its expressed goals not only the restoration of functioning within a practical life schema, but also addressing the theological aspects and implications of the critical incident and corresponding crisis response, in all instances (Hunter, 1990). Crisis chaplaincy, in practice, is the closest operational formulation to the notion of pastoral crisis intervention. The greatest difference is perhaps lexical, in that a chaplaincy most often denotes either a specialized form of pastoral care, or more commonly, pastoral care provided to a specialized group or organization, such as law enforcement, fire suppression, hospitals, the military, etc. (Hunter, 1990). Chaplaincy may also be seen as a pluralistic, non-doctrine, spiritually oriented intervention process.

Summary

In sum, *pastoral crisis intervention* may be defined as the functional integration of any and all religious, spiritual, faith-based, and pastoral resources with the assessment and intervention technologies germane to the practice of crisis intervention and disaster mental health. As previously noted, crisis intervention is to counseling and psychotherapy, as pastoral crisis intervention is to pastoral counseling and pastoral psychotherapy.

The goals of pastoral crisis intervention, as defined herein, are fundamentally the same as those of non-pastoral crisis intervention, i.e., the reduction of human distress, whether or not the distress concerns a significant loss, a crisis of meaning, a crisis of faith, or some far more concrete and objective infringement upon adaptive psychological functioning. In the context of this book, the pastoral orientation to crisis intervention brings with it a "value added" over and above the traditional non-pastoral approach to crisis intervention. This corpus of "value added" ingredients has been enumerated above as mechanisms of action, or agents of change, and appear to be unique to the pastoral perspective as it employs religious, spiritual, and theological resources in an effort to "shepherd" an individual from distress and dysfunction to restoration. As a result of these unique strengths, it seems clear that some form of pastoral crisis intervention option should be integrated within all critical incident stress management teams, community crisis response efforts (Community Emergency Response Teams, Community Emergency Response Networks), and disaster response systems.

Chapter Three

Recognition of Human Distress
with Rev. Thomas E. Webb

When I was 16 years old, I accompanied my associate pastor on a "house call." A member of our congregation wasextremely ditressed. She requested a "pastoral visitation." She felt that her distress could be best addressed from a faith-based perspective. The young minister did his best to reduce the distress experienced by the church member, relying upon what he later told me were basic helping skills and a pastoral presence. I wondered from that day forward how he knew that her distress could be best addressed from faith-based perspective and not a psychiatric one. Could it be that human distress, i.e., grief, guilt, depression, panic, and even psychosis, could be masked by a veneer of spiritual or religious turmoil? Could it be that spiritual or religious distress could be so severe so as to engender psychiatric consequences such as grief, guilt, depression, panic, and even psychosis? How is human distress manifest? Let us briefly review the nature of human distress.

□□□

The Nature of Human Stress

The term "stress" was first coined in the 1930s by Dr. Hans Selye, the greatest endocrinologist of his time, as well as the father of the "stress" concept. Selye thought of stress as "the sum total of wear and tear on the body." One of his colleagues, Paul Rosch thought of stress as "an acceleration of the aging process." Lastly, and perhaps most useful is a definition by Noble Laureate Walter Cannon who thought of stress as "the fight or flight response." Cannon's concept is very helpful because, more than other definitions, it actually tells us what the stress response was intended to do, i.e., to better prepare you to "fight" or to "flee" from a life threatening person or thing.

Stress, according to Selye in his classic book, *The Stress of Life*, has two primary variants: eustress and distress. Eustress is positive motivating stress. Distress is excessive stress that may lead to dysfunction and even mental and or physical illness. Selye emphatically noted that stress could not be avoided altogether, the absence of stress, he said, is death. Obviously, then, the goal in managing stress is to experience more eustress than distresss.

Physiology of stress

For our purposes, we will focus on the "fight or flight" physiology. In order to better prepare a person to fight or flee from a threat, the body releases numerous and varied physiology mechanisms. Everly and Lating (2002) describe three primary effector systems, or axes, for the expression of the human stress response:

1. Neural Axes
   a. Sympathetic nervous system
   b. Parasympathetic nervous system
   c. Neuromuscular nervous system
2. Neuroendocrine Axes
   a. Adrenal medullary release of adrenalin into the systemic blood circulation
   b. Adrenal medullary release of noradrenalin into the systemic blood circulation
3. Endocrine Axes
   a. Adrenal cortical release of cortisol into the systemic circulation (cortisol is a glucocorticoid hormone that increases blood sugar while reducing immunity)
   b. Adrenal cortical release of aldosterone into the systemic circulation (aldosterone is a mineralocorticoid hormone that causes sodium retention and therefore fluid retention)
   c. Alterations in thyroidal hormones leading to hyperthyroidism or hypothyroidism-like reactions
   d. Alterations in human growth hormone
   e. Alterations in gonadotropic hormones (such alterations may affect reproductive-related behavior)

Many of these reactions are actually designed to enhance the chances of physical survival when confronted by a life-threatening situation. Interestingly though, most of the stressful situations that modern era humans face have nothing to do with life-threatening challenges. When these effector systems are activated for prolonged periods, they can become pathogenic.

Problems can arise in a host of bodily systems, yielding results such as:

1. increased serum lipids
2. increased blood pressure
3. irregular heart rhythms
4. vasospastic syndromes, such as migraine headaches and Raynaud's disease
5. either increased immune responsiveness, resulting in autoimmune diseases, or decreased immune responses, resulting in vulnerability to infectious diseases
6. gastrointestinal problems, such as colitis, irritable bowel syndromes, and ulcers
7. neuromuscular syndromes such as tension headaches and muscle spasms
8. dermatologic syndromes
9. sexual dysfunction

Psychology of stress

We return to Hans Selye to help us better understand the psychology of stress. Selye once noted, "It is not what happens to you that matters, but how you take it." Perhaps the most acclaimed pioneer in the field of psychosomatic medicine, Stuart Wolf, once said, "It is evident from the idiosyncratic nature of interpreting experience that to understand the impact of an event, the focus of inquiry must be the individual." The philosopher Epictetus once wrote that man is disturbed, not by things, but by the views which he takes of them. Even Shakespeare once wrote, "For there are no things good nor bad, but thinking makes them so." Finally, it was once suggested that stressors, like beauty, lie in the eye of the beholder. What do all of these statements have in common? The answer, we believe, is that most of the stress in one's life comes about because of how one views the people, places, and things in the world around them. The meanings that one assigns to things are the essential determinants of happiness, and even effectiveness as a worker, a spouse, and a parent.

Excessive Stress (Distress)

If one can recognize the "early warning" signs of excessive stress, one may be better prepared to manage these reactions before they become incapacitating. The signs and symptoms of distress may appear in one or more forms:

1. COGNITIVE (Thinking)
    - Sensory distortion
    - Inability to concentrate
    - Difficulty in decision making
    - Guilt
    - Preoccupation (obsessions) with event
    - Confusion ("dumbing down")
    - Inability to understand consequences of behavior
2. EMOTIONAL
    - Anxiety
    - Irritability
    - Anger
    - Mood swings
    - Depressed mood
    - Fear, phobia, phobic avoidance
    - Grief
3. BEHAVIORAL
    - Impulsiveness
    - Risk-taking
    - Excessive eating
    - Alcoholor drug use
    - Hyperstartle
    - Compensatory sexuality
    - Sleep disturbance
    - Withdrawal
    - Family discord
    - Crying spells
    - Hypervigilance, suspiciousness
4. PHYSICAL
    - Tachycardia or Bradycardia

- Headaches
- Hyperventilation
- Muscle spasms
- Psychogenic sweating
- Fatigue/exhaustion
- Indigestion, nausea, vomiting

5. SPIRITUAL
   - Anger at God
   - Withdrawal from Faith-based community
   - Crisis of Faith

Extreme distress may show itself in many ways, here are four of the most common clinical examples for which people seek formal psychological care.

Burnout

Burnout may be thought of as mental, and sometimes physical, exhaustion. Burnout is sometimes related to what some have called the "midlife crisis," or "mid-career crisis." It should be noted that the midlife crisis can occur at any point in your life, and may actually occur more than once (ages 40 and 50 are common ages for these symptoms to arise).

The classic signs and symptoms of the "burnout syndrome" may include, but are not limited to:

- chronic negativism
- cynicism
- anger
- second guessing yourself and others
- lateness
- incomplete projects
- a decay in the quality of work performed on the job
- a resentment of supervisors, even clients
- extramarital affairs
- increased risk taking
- a sense of desperation that life is slipping away

- a general dissatisfaction with life, family, career
- the desire to relocate geographically
- the desire to change careers
- the desire to divorce
- increased alcohol and/or tobacco use
- depression
- panic attacks
- a fear of aging
- dressing and acting much "younger"
- a sense of a foreshortened future
- In the most extreme variations, it may be associated with suicidal, even homicidal, thoughts.

Panic

A panic attack is best thought of as a discrete paroxysmal interval of intense fear, psychological discomfort, and extreme psychophysiological arousal. Psychological/behavioral symptoms of panic often include:

- the belief that one is dying
- extreme fear
- uncertainty
- hopelessness
- a sense of acute environmental constriction
- possible phobia formation

Physiological symptoms can be diverse and remarkably varied between individuals. They may include, but not be limited to:

- sweating
- cardiac palpitations
- tachycardia
- bradycardia
- nausea
- vertigo
- hyperventilation

Depression

Everyone gets "sad." Some people get depressed. What is the difference? Think of sadness on one end of a continuum and clinical depression on then other. You are likely to get sad if you have a "bad" day. You are likely to get sad if someone or something disappoints you. Depression, on the other hand, is more commonly associated with loss. The loss could be the loss of a personal relationship, or the loss could be the loss of something that you consider important, such as a job, money, status, even an opportunity. The loss could even be the loss of hope or the loss of a sense of a future. When depression becomes severe, certain rather predictable signs and symptoms emerge.

The primary *psychological* symptoms of clinical depression include:
- depressed mood
- emptiness, or sense of irreplaceable loss
- anhedonia
- hopelessness
- helplessness, and sometimes
- suicidal ideation.

The classic *physical* symptoms of depression include:
- loss of appetite
- weight loss potential
- diminished libido
- terminal insomnia (sleep maintenance insomnia)
- psychomotor retardation
- diminished energy.

Posttraumatic Stress Disorder (PTSD)

This psychiatric disorder was first officially introduced in the Diagnostic and Statistical Manual of Mental Disorders, Third Edition, published by the American Psychiatric Association in 1980. The 1994 revision of that diagnostic taxonomy indicates that PTSD is a rather predictable sequelae of symptoms that lie in the wake of psychological trauma (the most severe form of human stressor). A traumatic event involves the threat of, or actual, physical injury or death (although earlier conceptualizations considered a traumatic event as anything outside the usual realm of human experience that would be markedly distressing to anyone). Its key features include three symptom clusters subsequent to the exposure to a traumatic event:

1. intrusive memories and recollections of the traumatic event in the form of persistent and distressing dreams, flashbacks, and/or intrusive thoughts/images;
2. persistent avoidance of and withdrawal from people, places, and/or things associated with the traumatic event, as well as depressive symptoms;
3. persistent symptoms of increased arousal, such as hyperstartle reactions, irritability, angry outbursts, and sleep disturbance.

In the book, *Personality-Guided Therapy for Posttraumatic Stress Disorder,* the authors, George S. Everly, Jr. and Jeffrey M. Lating (2004), analyzed the posttraumatic stress disorder construct and found it to reveal two key components or constituents:

- neurologic hypersensitivity and
- psychologic hypersensitivity.

The neurologic hypersensitivity is thought to consist of a lowered depolarization threshold deep within the center of the brain, an area known as the amygdaloid posterior hypothalamic efferent pathways of the limbic system. This functional hypersensitivity is thought to give rise to a potential over-reactive cascade, such as behavioral impulsivity, irritability, and propensity for violence.

The psychologic hypersensitivity is thought to arise from a violation of some deeply held belief. This belief is referred to as a worldview. Thus, a traumatic event, according to this perspective, is predicated upon some situation that violates a deeply-held and important worldview. There appear to be five core beliefs that, when violated, give rise to posttraumatic stress reactions.

- Violation of the belief that the world is "just" or "fair." Thus, why does an infant die in a motor vehicle accident?
- Guilt and a violation of your sense of self-esteem and character, in effect a violation of the sense of who you are by having not done something you should, or by having done something you should not have done.

- Abandonment, betrayal, violation of trust. Betrayal by a parent, family member, trusted friend, or even a spouse.
- Violation of a sense of safety, universally speaking. Something may occur that makes the world seem like an unsafe place.
- Violation of some sense of coherency, e.g., religion, spirituality, science, etc. Some trauma may take away the "glue" that holds the world together from the context of making sense (sometimes considered an explanatory worldview).

When one or more of these beliefs are seriously threatened or violated/contradicted, it is not uncommon to experience posttraumatic stress reactions. If these reactions interfere with one's ability to function on a daily basis (at work and/or at home), then we refer to it as a stress disorder.

Compassion Fatigue

Dr. Charles Figley has observed that it may be possible to develop a form of PTSD simply by helping those who have been traumatized. Compassion fatigue—or secondary traumatic stress disorder—is the natural consequence of stress, resulting from caring for and helping traumatized people, or even animals. This form of stress occurs when professionals become so overwhelmed that they themselves experience feelings of fear, pain, and suffering. They may suffer from reactions similar to the form of PTSD we just discussed, such as, intrusive thoughts, nightmares, loss of energy, and perception of threats at home or at work.

Potential Markers for Psychological Triage

The following factors should be considered when considering the disposition of anyone in acute distress. Factors 1 through 8 are predictors of posttraumatic stress disorder (PTSD). Factors 9 through 11 warrant immediate intervention and referral for continued, higher order care.

1. Peri-traumatic dissociation. Did the person experience a dissociative episode as the stressful event was taking place?
2. Peri-traumatic depression
3. Peri-traumatic belief one was going to die
4. Catastrophically negative appraisal of symptoms
5. Physical injuries
6. Peri-traumatic panic

7. Psychogenic amnesia
8. Peri-traumatic depression, despair, numbing
9. Homicidal ideation
10. Suicidal ideation
11. Psychosis
12. Finally, consider what was the precipitating event that caused the psychological distress? If it was a traumatic event, we know that there is a dose - response relationship with exposure to extremely stressful events and the subsequent development of psychiatric disorders.

The Challenges of Hearing a Spiritual Cry of Distress

How does one distinguish a cry of distress in spiritual or religious semantic versus a true crisis of faith? How does one distinguish a crisis of faith from a candid, but painful, plea to God? The first step in answering that question requires the pastoral interventionist to accept that for religious persons will often express themselves using religious language from their faith tradition. Their communication of distress reflects a normal mode of expressing grief congruent with their faith perspective. Thus, a differential diagnostic challenge becomes distinguishing the following three reactions that may be often confused:

1. The use of spiritual or religious semantics to express what is really psychological distress.
2. The challenge of theodicy, wherein the person in crisis expresses a question to God in some effort to gain respite from agonizing psychological pain, such as grief. The theodolitic question is often posed, " How could my benevolent God allow this to happen?" Herein the person is asking a question in order to understand God's will. Through understanding, a sense of relief may be obtained.
3. Finally, the crisis of faith represents the most severe form of theodolitic and pastoral crisis, wherein the foundations of religious belief are not just shaken but eroded and collapsing.

Having an assessment algorithm will guide interventionists in making statements that connect with the impaired individual to whom they are speaking. Without such a method of discernment, the well-meaning interventionist may default to whatever seems familiar in their primary professional identity as a peer, clergy member, or therapist and respond to initial spiritual cries of distress and the disturbing comments of a crisis of faith with comments that miss the mark.

- The use of spiritual or religious semantics in and of themselves does not indicate a crisis of theodicy. Listen carefully. Religious semantics may simply be used as a form of semantic explanation point.

- When there is indeed a theodolitic crisis, the most common mistake that may be made is to try to "solve" the theodolitic dilemma in the moment of crisis.

- To begin, ask how the individual would desire to "understand" or "justify" the occurrence. That is, what "explanation" would be most comforting to them. Affirm such a conclusion as best you can (if you can) and support that interpretation, at least in the acute phase.

- In circumstances where there is no "most comforting" explanation, consider reliance upon faith (acceptance), while delaying the need to "understand" until referral for pastoral guidance/ counseling can be achieved.

Keep in mind that a crisis of faith occurs when one's normal, established relationship with God and accompanying theological world view is violated and seemingly rendered helpless and/or useless in making sense of relationships with God and others (Webb, 2001). In light of this definition, a pastoral crisis interventionist faces the daunting tasks of hearing accurately the spiritual cry of distress and establishing a context within which to assess the statement and symptoms of the person in distress. Religious cries of distress often evoke an intense sense of helplessness and despair within the listening crisis interventionist. Several questions arise for the interventionist seeking to provide spiritual crisis care including, "Where do I start? On what do I focus? Do I need to learn the person's religious language before I can make a strategic spiritual intervention?"

For example, a mother holding her newly stillborn baby looks up and remorsefully sobs, "My baby is dead! How could God let my baby die?" The saddened tear-filled eyes and the mother's words communicate powerfully and can evoke within the interventionist shock, agony, and the loneliness of the moment. At this point the interventionist must maintain balance and perspective so as to be able to make a response that reflects that they have accurately heard the cry of sorrowful distress. Being attentive and remaining silent for a few moments are non-verbal ways of communicating support in a moment where an over-abundance of words would be distracting and unhelpful. The interventionist's silent and attentive presence can honor the moment of pain and the severity of the loss but so also can a timely spoken word such as, "I am so saddened for you. Your child's death seems heartbreaking."

Careful discernment needs to be applied in assessing this powerful theological expression of spiritual distress. The theological language of the mother reflects her extreme sense of helplessness, shock, and horror. It portrays a snapshot of her current spiritual state of being overwhelmed.

The emergence of the following kinds of spiritual traumatic stress symptoms characterize an individual experiencing a crisis of faith.

1. Sense of being abandoned by God (a sense of disruption of relationship)

2. Difficulty in praying (a sense of breakdown in communication and connectedness)

3. No yearning for righteousness (a sense of confusion with respect to one's purpose in life)

4. No spirit of thankfulness (a sense of a loss of joy and purpose for living)

5. No sense of hope (a sense of isolation and despairing helplessness)

Without intervention, initial expressions of spiritual distress may grow and fulminate to a state of spiritual impairment in one's relationship with God.

In the time frame and context of a crisis of faith, the following statements (identical in wording to the initial cries of distress) focus on the individual's disruption, discord, distance, and confusion in their relationship with God:

- "How could God let this awful thing happen?"
- "I am so angry with God!"
- "Why does God not hear my prayers?"
- "O my God, where are you?"
- "Why do you stand so far off, O Lord?"
- "Why, Lord, do you hide yourself in times of trouble?"

As a crisis interventionist interacts with one who is experiencing a crisis of faith, the interventionist will confront an emotionally and spiritually charged environment reflective of such statements. Some common potent symptoms that get conveyed to the interventionist include the following:

- a sense of being lost and uncertain due to feeling as if God has abandoned them
- a lack of desire to seek intimacy with God through prayer
- a sense of apathy regarding pursuing a righteous life
- a loss of a sense of thankfulness and hope
- a lack of comfort and support from reading and meditating on the Scriptures
- a sense of apathy to continue relationships with fellow faith members

As one patiently sits with the person in their spiritual distress, the interventionist needs to listen actively to their cry of distress and give opportunity for their expression and confession of a spectrum of emotions and confusion. Indeed, the expressions of anger, fear, helplessness, hopelessness, and a desire for things to be the way they used to be can be quite intense and unnerving. In the process of actively listening and paraphrasing back to the individual, the interventionist serves as an ambassador and present witness of God's faithfulness and love.

The Challenge of Remaining in the Role of a Pastoral Crisis Interventionist

Events such as the stillbirth of a child are vastly incongruent to the joyful expectation of birth with which a mother and father enter the hospital. This stark incongruence between the expectation of joy and the shocking outcome of death exacerbates the impact of the traumatic stress. Further fueling the severity of the trauma in the spiritual context is the puzzling and shocking dilemma of how an Almighty God could "let my innocent baby die." In a time of crisis, a pastoral crisis interventionist faces the temptation to shift from their role as a crisis interventionist to the role with which they are more familiar. Without conscious effort to maintain one's balance and perspective in this moment, a crisis interventionist may easily be ensnared and enmeshed in the expression of anxiety and despair. In this intervention context, the crisis care provider will feel a strong temptation to want to "fix" the spiritual crisis of the individual. Pastors will be tempted to preach. Clergy and chaplains are tempted to give a highly cognitive, theological response to somehow answer the question of why God could let this happen. Counselors will be tempted to counsel. And therapists will be tempted to conduct a therapy session. However, the crisis interventionist needs to focus on being present with the impacted individual as they traverse their spiritual valley of the shadow of death. To aid a person in getting restored to functioning with hope and thankfulness in their relationship with God, the interventionist needs to meet the individual where they are.

Summary

In this chapter, the challenge of the differential assessment has been introduced. The assessment process must not only consider the theodolitic challenges, but must consider the psychiatric, as well. It is well known that extreme human stress and even frank psychiatric discord will masquerade as spiritual or religious expressions. We will see later that crisis intervention should be focused upon a rapid and accurate assessment of need with the subsequent intention of stabilization and acute mitigation of distress. Pastoral crisis intervention is not therapy, nor pastoral counseling, nor is it a substitute for same.

□□□

Chapter Four

A Model for Pastoral Crisis Intervention

☐☐☐

The term *pastoral crisis intervention* has been defined as the functional integration of faith-based resources with traditional crisis intervention assessment and intervention technologies. Pastoral crisis intervention has been differentiated from ministry and the provision of chaplaincy services. Given the apparent natural affinity that many individuals show for faith-based support, guidance, and/or reassurance, it is interesting, indeed, to note historically the conspicuous omission of faith-based resources as part of a "formalized" community-wide crisis intervention and disaster response. Such services have traditionally been supplied within the context of chaplaincy services to well-circumscribed groups, but have usually lacked breadth in large-scale community crises. Pastoral counseling services have certainly been used in the wake of community crises and disasters, but these are, by definition, "counseling services" and not "crisis intervention." As noted by Everly (Everly & Mitchell, 1999), crisis intervention is very different compared to counseling and psychotherapy. As described by Everly, crisis intervention may be considered a form of psychological "first-aid." The goals of crisis intervention are to

1. stabilize signs and symptoms of distress and dysfunction,

2. mitigate signs and symptoms of distress and dysfunction,

3. facilitate a return to adaptive functioning, or

4. seek continued care, typically a higher level of care.

Everly (2000a) has offered the term "pastoral crisis intervention" as the functional integration of any and all religious, spiritual, and pastoral resources with the assessment and intervention technologies typically thought of as crisis intervention. Thus, pastoral crisis intervention may be seen as a "value added" form of crisis intervention. In this chapter, we shall look at a structure for the provision of pastoral crisis intervention.

Active Ingredients and a Value Added

When pastoral crisis intervention is effective, what makes it so? Table 1 enumerates the active ingredients in crisis intervention, including those value-added ingredients unique to pastoral crisis intervention.

Table 1
Active Mechanisms of Crisis Intervention (from Everly, 2000a)

Psychological Mechanisms

1. Early Intervention
2. Cathartic Ventilation
3. Social Support, a supportive and genuine presence
4. Problem-Solving
5. Conflict Resolution
6. Cognitive Reinterpretation/ Reframing
7. Liaison/ Advocacy
8. Instillation of Hope

Spiritual and Religious "Value-added" Mechanisms Unique to Pastoral Crisis Intervention

1. "Ministry of Presence," and the Unique Ethos of the Pastoral Crisis Interventionist
2. Scriptural Education, Insight, Reinterpretation
3. Individual and Conjoint Prayer
4. Intercessory Prayer
5. Unifying and Explanatory Worldviews
6. Ventilative Confession
7. Faith-Based Social Support Systems
8. Rituals and Sacraments
9. Belief in Divine Intervention/Forgiveness
10. Belief in a Life after Death
11. Uniquely Confidential/Privileged Communications
12. Instillation of Hope based upon Spiritual or Religious Foundations

Note: Depending upon the specific belief, more or fewer of these mechanisms may be active.

Pastoral Crisis Intervention Functionally Defined

As we look at the process of pastoral crisis intervention, it may be of value to begin to shape an intervention plan or structure. A first step in this process would be to compartmentalize the various functional processes contained within pastoral crisis intervention. As we review Table 1, the following functional categories would seem to emerge:

1. *Assessment* - Evaluation of mental, behavioral, spiritual, and religious status, so as to determine need for intervention

2. *Psychological intervention* - Use of basic, generic psychological principles to mitigate acute distress

3. *Liaison/Advocacy intervention* - Serving the person in crisis as an intermediary or advocate, wherein one serves to buffer the person from further stressors, and/or assists the person in obtaining access to further resources and services

4. *Spiritual intervention* - Use of pastoral interventions generically applicable across religions / faiths; including Spiritual First Aid

5. *Religious intervention* - Use of pastoral interventions based upon specific religious doctrine, belief, or scripture

Putting it all Together: The SAFER-R Model of Pastoral Crisis Intervention

Effective crisis response is predicated upon knowledge and skill. While no two crises will be exactly the same, it is usually helpful to work within a framework, to follow a somewhat structured course, a "psychological roadmap" or protocol, during the process of one's crisis response intervention. *See Figure 1.*

The SAFER-Revised model represents a protocol for conducting individual crisis response interventions. As such, it may be a useful psychological roadmap to follow as one assists an individual in crisis.

Uses: The SAFER-R model is designed for use with individuals in crisis. The SAFER-R model may be used on-scene during an acute crisis or disaster situation, or anywhere and at anytime after the initial impact.

Goals: The goals of the SAFER-R model are those of most acute crisis response protocols, i.e., to mitigate the acute distress of the individual in crisis and to facilitate access to follow-up mental health assessment and treatment, if needed.

Format: The SAFER-R model follows a specific progression of stages. The stages of the model are as follows.

Figure 1
**SAFER-Revised Model of Pastoral Crisis
Intervention With Individuals**

Stabilization (plus Introduction) [1]

Acknowledgement [1]
Events
Reactions

Facilitation of Understanding: Normalization [1]

Encourage Effective Coping (PCI Mechanisms of Action) [1,2,3]
Psychological
Liaison, Advocacy
Spiritual
Religious

Referral? [1,2,3]

*[1 = Assessment, 2 = Generate intervention options,
3 = Implement Interventions]*

Stabilization of the Situation or Response

In this initial step in the SAFER protocol, the crisis interventionist assesses the impact that the immediate environment is having on the person in crisis and acts to remove the person from any provocative stressors (people or things) that may be sustaining the crisis. This can be achieved by first introducing oneself and asking what assistance might be provided:

"This seems really hard, how can I help?"

"What can I do for now that might be of some assistance?"

"What do you need right now?"

"You look like you're having a hard time, how can I be of assistance?"

Things like "taking a walk," "getting a cup of coffee," or any other diversionary process that provides the individual with some "psychological distance" from the source of the acute crisis or any other situation may be of assistance. Prior to any such intervention, however, the crisis interventionist must always introduce him /herself and the role that is being served or performed.

Acknowledgment of the Crisis

The second step in the SAFER intervention is the acknowledgment of the crisis itself. This stage is fostered by a skillful use of basic helping communication techniques. In this stage, the crisis interventionist asks the person in crisis to describe "what happened" to create the crisis situation. The specific wording will of course depend upon the response in the previous stage.

"Can you tell me what happened?"

"What can you tell me about what happened?"

Because a crisis is often punctuated by escalating emotions, this question gives the person in a crisis a cue and reason to return to the cognitive thinking domain, at least temporarily. Yet it is not usually advised to discourage cathartic ventilation, unless the emotions are escalating out of control. Therefore, after having described the nature of the crisis situation, the person in crisis is asked to describe his/her current state of psychological functioning. A simple prompt such as, "How are you doing now?" allows the person who is in crisis to return to cathartic ventilation, but now in a somewhat more structured and secure manner. Thus, we see within this stage, the crisis interventionist has superimposed cognitive oriented communications over the potentially labile emotional foundation. Later, however, having listened to the nature of the crisis, the interventionist encourages emotional ventilation in a safer, more structured communication environment.

Facilitation of Understanding

The third stage in the present model involves a transition back to the cognitive psychological domain for the person in crisis. In this third stage, the crisis interventionist begins to actively respond to the information revealed by the person in crisis during the previous stage. Here the person in crisis is encouraged to view his/her reactions to the crisis as generally "normal" (if indeed that is the case), expected reactions being experienced by a "normal" individual, in response to an abnormally challenging situation (i.e., a crisis situation). The primary goals of this stage of the SAFER model are:

- to assist the person in crisis in returning to the cognitive domain of psychological processing and

- to encourage the person in crisis to see his/her symptoms as basically "normal" reactions to an extraordinarily stressful event, thus dispelling the myth of unique vulnerability or weakness. This, of course, assumes that the symptoms presented are "normal" and non-malignant in nature.

Encourage Adaptive Coping

The fourth stage of the model represents what is usually the most overtly active stage with regard to the behavior of the crisis interventionist. Here the pastoral interventionist employs the "active ingredients" enumerated in Table 1.

It is within this fourth stage that the crisis interventionist will consider facilitating:

- various "self-curing" abilities of individuals in crisis (further understanding, mastery, and self-enhancement), and

- active psychological or behavioral interventions (e.g., ventilation, problem-solving/conflict resolution, and cognitive reevaluation, pastoral interventions).

"Self-curing" abilities of individuals

Taylor (1983), in the context of her studies on victimization, has written cogently on the ability of the human psyche to naturally recover from adversity. She notes, "These self-curing abilities are a formidable resource..." (Taylor, 1983, p. 1161). Not only are they important social psychological characteristics to understand as part of crisis and victim phenomenology, but they are important dynamic healing forces that may prove of great value if harnessed and/or augmented by the crisis interventionist. But, in order to be effectively harnessed, or augmented, the crisis interventionist must first understand their nature. Taylor suggests three self-curing forces exist.

1. *Gaining a sense of understanding* with regard to the experience.

Recovery is facilitated as the person in crisis discovers reasonable and functional answers to these commonly asked questions:

    a. What caused this crisis to occur?

    b. What personal meaning does this event now have for the person in crisis?

2. *Gaining a sense of mastery* over the event and one's life in the wake of the crisis. Recovery is facilitated as the person in crisis discovers reasonable and functional answers to these commonly asked questions:

    a. What can be done to control the crisis event?

    b. How can the adverse reaction to the event be mitigated?

    c. How can the crisis be avoided in the future?

3. *Gaining a sense of self-enhancement* from the crisis event.

According to Taylor, self-enhancement is often achieved through a process of comparison. Taylor (1983) suggest that there are five commonly used comparative strategies:

1. Comparing oneself with other crisis victims who experienced less fortunate outcomes (downward comparison).

2. Focusing on one selective aspect of the crisis event, or a specific outcome, that would allow the victim to seem advantageous.

3. Creating hypothetical worse case scenarios ("It could have been worse.")

4. Recognition of some beneficial outcome attributed to the crisis event.

5. Recognition that the rate of personal recovery is exceptional compared to others, or that which would be expected.

Psychological and behavioral interventions

Specific psychological and behavioral goals will vary from person to person and crisis to crisis, but there are generic psychological and behavioral processes that commonly prove useful in crisis situations:

- Early intervention
- Cathartic ventilation/victim self-disclosure.
- Problem solving/conflict resolution.
- Social support

- The "cognitive key," cognitive restructuring.
- Liaison
- Advocacy
- Hope

Early Intervention

Crisis interventions are designed to be implemented during the acute crisis phase, i.e., in-the-field on-scene support, as quickly after the acute crisis event as possible, or as predicated upon the emergence of a crisis reaction no matter when. There is simply nothing quicker by design. Early, if not immediate, intervention has long been recognized as an important aspect of crisis response.

Salmon (1919) and Artiss (1963) noted the importance of rapid, emergency-oriented psychiatric intervention in World War I and World War II, respectively.

Lindy's (1985) notion of the trauma membrane argues that after a traumatic event victims begin to "insulate" themselves from the world through the construction of a "trauma membrane," or protective shell. The longer one waits to penetrate the shell, the more difficult it becomes, according to this formulation.

Earlier, Rapoport (1965) argued for the practical importance of early intervention, as did Spiegel and Classen (1995) in their review of emergency psychiatry.

Empirically, Bordow and Porritt (1979) were probably the first to test the importance of early crisis response. Their results support the conclusion that immediate intervention is more effective than delayed intervention.

Solomon and Benbenishty (1986) empirically analyzed the three tenets of crisis response: immediacy, proximity, and expectancy. Each of the three was found to exert a positive effect. That effect was seen to last 20 years longitudinally (Solomon, et al., 2005)

Lastly, Post (1992), in a most provocative paper, argues that early intervention may prevent a genetically-based lowered threshold for neurological excitation from developing in response to trauma. Thus, early intervention may prevent the development of a cellular "memory" of trauma from being transmitted to excitatory neural tissues.

Cathartic Ventilation and Self-disclosure

It is now abundantly clear that the processes of cathartic ventilation and self-disclosure are powerful therapeutic forces. Pennebaker (1985, 1990,

1999) has elegantly investigated the therapeutic value inherent in the processes of both written and verbal disclosure. Simply stated, there appear to be powerful psychotherapeutic, physiologic, and behavioral consequences to the process of disclosing about traumatic events. The crisis interventionist should keep in mind that merely allowing the person in crisis to "ventilate" may be sufficient to stabilize symptoms of distress and allow the individual to restore some level of independent functioning. In other cases, the act of self-disclosure merely serves as a necessary prerequisite to more specific content-oriented problem solving. It has been said that emotions often serve as barriers to effective problem solving and, as such, must be addressed before meaningful problem solving can be attempted.

Problem Solving and Conflict Resolution

Obviously, the most powerful form of crisis intervention is that which results in the removal, or direct mitigation, of the stressor that caused the crisis to initially emerge. Sir Francis Bacon once said that information is power. In some instances, the crisis interventionist will either possess relevant information, or will know how to access relevant information that will prove of value to the person in crisis as methods of problem solving and conflict resolution are explored. In such instances, the crisis interventionist becomes a valuable content resource for the person in crisis.

Semantically, as well as practically, problem-solving and conflict resolution may be viewed as somewhat different types of crisis resolution techniques. It will be of value to differentiate the two.

Problem Solving - Most commonly, we view problem solving in the context of attempting to resolve, or remove, an unwanted stressor which, ostensibly, lies at the root of the acute crisis. The nature and adverse impact of the stressor is usually quite clear to the person in crisis, as well as the crisis interventionist. Directive, action-oriented interventions often prove quite useful. Unfortunately, a mistake that is often made by individuals experiencing this type of crisis is to prematurely flee the situation, for example, quitting a job, obtaining a divorce, moving across town or country, or even resorting to violence as a means of removing the stressor. The key elements that discriminate effective from ineffective problem solving are 1) the directiveness and specificity of the intervention, 2) the timing of the intervention, and 3) realistic assessment of the consequences of one's responses in the crisis situation. Perhaps the most common mistake that people in crisis make is to fail to realistically assess the impact, or consequences, of their actions. The crisis interventionist can play a powerful role by merely providing objective feedback regarding the consequences of various crisis resolution options. Sometimes the best option is to simply wait.

Conflict Resolution - Conflict resolution, on the other hand, represents another form of crisis intervention, which is different than direct problem solving. Conflict resolution denotes, not so much the presence of a unilateral and well-circumscribed stressor, but rather denotes a conflict of two or more intentions, presences, or actions, all of which may be quite legitimate and functional in and of themselves. The "problem" inherent in the process of conflict resolution is the relationship between the factors which make up the conflict. Typically, the most salient dynamic in a conflict is the incompatibility of intentions, presences, or actions. Thus, the task at hand for the crisis interventionist in the context of conflict resolution becomes finding a compromise wherein a "win-win" condition may emerge. By "win-win" we mean an outcome that is acceptable to all, even though it may not be 100% of what was intended by any of the parties. Through compromise, all of the conflicted parties can extract some sense of success from the conflict resolution process. The challenge for the crisis interventionist is listening carefully and planning innovatively enough so as to construct the "win-win" environment. It is important to understand that the "win-win" resolution may have to be a temporary one that merely allows for subsequent, and more permanent, conflict resolution. While it is clear that problem solving and conflict resolution can be powerful crisis intervention techniques, they are not always practical in the acute crisis situation.

Cognitive Restructuring

While efforts to control one's environment through problem solving can be a powerful intervention when conditions allow, it may leave one with feelings of helplessness when such tactics fail. Many people in crisis experience such reactions because they fail to understand that while controlling the environment can be a powerful stress reduction tactic, so too can exerting control over how one thinks about, or interprets, the environment and the events in one's life. Learning to view a crisis situation from a less stressful, more ego syntonic, perspective is another process that facilitates recovery. Taplin (1971) offered an early cognitive perspective on crisis intervention. This author argued that the essential element in a crisis situation is how the person perceives, or interprets, the crisis event. This view is consistent with Everly's (1989) comprehensive model of the human stress response, as well as his view of the etiology of posttraumatic stress disorder (Everly & Lating, 2004). Pennebaker (1999) concluded that much of the power of ventilation was in allowing individuals to cognitively analyze the crisis, or problem. A crisis results when a new situation arises that cannot be understood or effectively managed via customary mechanisms of understanding and/or coping. Such a conceptualization of the crisis condition leads to its natural therapeutic corollary, i.e., some form of cognitive restructuring. Cognitive restructuring is the act of changing one's view, or interpretation, of a situation so as to reduce its distressing impact. While often used in psychotherapy, it is also a useful, "common sense" approach to crisis situations that are not amenable to problem solving. As Taylor (1983) points out, this is a powerful, self-initiated, approach that many individuals naturally employ in the wake of adversity.

The Provision of Psychosocial Support

All human beings require some form of support from others (i.e., psychosocial support). Such support may come in the form of esteem, friendship, respect, trust, aid in problem-solving, or merely listening. Crisis accentuates this need.

American psychologist Carl Rogers wrote cogently in his theory of self psychology that all humans have an innate need for "positive regard" (Rogers, 1951). They possess a need to be valued by others.

Bowlby (1969) argues that there exists a biological drive for the bonding, or attachment, between humans, especially between mother and child.

Similarly, Maslow (1970) has written most coherently that one of the basic human needs is the need for social affiliation with others. According to Maslovian theory, many crises result from a loss of social support/affiliation.

Jerome Frank (1974), in his analysis of psychotherapy, argues that all psychotherapeutic improvement is based on the intervention's ability to reduce demoralization, especially through contradicting the notion of alienation. Individuals in crisis often feel alone, uniquely plagued, and abandoned.

By its very existence, any form of crisis response initiates the process of social support. It contradicts the alienation phenomenon, shows caring, and shows that the person in crisis is valued by others. It also contradicts any sense of abandonment.

The empirical evidence for social support as an effective crisis response tactic is persuasive. Buckley, Blanchard, and Hickling (1996) found an inverse relationship between social support and the prevalence of posttraumatic stress disorder in the wake of motor vehicle accidents. Bunn and Clarke (1979), in an early study of crisis intervention technologies, found that as crisis counseling services were provided, in the form of 20 minutes of supportive counseling, anxiety levels diminished. Dalgleish, and others (1996) also confirmed the assumption that social support is inversely correlated with posttraumatic stress-related symptoms. Finally, Flannery (1990), in a comprehensive review of the role of social support in psychological trauma, found a general trend indicative of the value of social support in reducing the adverse impact of trauma.

Liaison - Sometimes intervention simply consists of serving as a bridge for the person in crisis thereby connecting them to supportive people and resources.

Advocacy - In some instances, intervention takes on an active advocacy role attempting to secure resources that might not otherwise be available to the person in crisis or their family.

Hope - The ultimate goal of any and all of these interventions is the instillation of hope.

Pastoral Interventions

It is at this point in the SAFER-R model that the unique vale-added interventions of spirituality and religion would be largely applied. These were enumerated in Table 1.

1. Spiritual Interventions
    a. Unique Ethos of Pastoral Person
    b. Ministry of Presence
    c. Unique Communication
    d. Ventilative Confession
    e. Individual and/or Conjoint Prayer
    f. Belief in Divine Order or Divine Intervention

2. Religious Interventions
    a. Scriptural Education, Insight, Interpretation
    b. Rituals, Sacraments
    c. Rituals of Forgiveness, Atonement
    d. Prayer

These are obviously applied in such a manner so as to match the intervention with the assessed spiritual or religious needs of the person in crisis, but again, the individual or collective power of these interventions resides in the instillation of hope.

In Tables 2 and 3 we see indications for the use of spiritual and/or religious interventions (Table 2) and potential "problems with using the pastoral approach to crisis intervention" (Table 3).

Restoration Of Adaptive, Independent Functioning, or Referral

The goal of the previous four stages is always to assist the person in reestablishing adaptive, independent psychological and behavioral functioning. In the vast majority of cases, this will have been achieved by this point in the process. In some instances, however, it will be evident that the person in crisis is remaining in a highly unstable condition. If such is the case, the crisis interventionist's goal becomes that of providing assistance in obtaining continued acute care. Resources for such continued care might be family members, the clergy, organizational resources, or, in extreme cases where no other resources seem suitable, an emergency room, or even law enforcement authorities.

Table 2
Indications for the Utilization of the Pastoral Crisis Intervention Mechanisms

1. Receptive Expectations, i.e., the expectation/desire on the part of the person(s) in crisis for prayer, scriptural guidance, provision of sacraments, rituals, etc.

2. Receptive State of Mind, i.e., while not specifically "expecting" such interventions, the person(s) in crisis is "open," or psychologically receptive, to pastoral intervention. It is important that argumentation, or debate, be avoided in the acute crisis state. Such actions tend to make the interventionist part of the "problem" not part of the "solution."

3. Pastoral crisis intervention can, obviously, be employed with not only primary victims of crisis, but with family members, emergency response personnel, observers, etc., but the same guidelines listed above would be applicable.

Table 3
**Potential Problems in the Application of Pastoral
Crisis Intervention**

1. Failure to "listen" to the secular needs of the person in crisis.
2. Lack of a structured intervention plan, or approach, to the person in crisis.
3. Arguing or debating spiritual/theological issues with the person in acute crisis.
4. Attempting to explain spiritually/theologically "why" a trauma occurred.
5. Preaching or praying with the "unreceptive" individual.
6. Attempting to "convert" the unreceptive individual.
7. Difficulty in the differentiation of clinical signs/symptoms, for example:
   a. Major depression vs. grief reaction
   b. Brief psychotic reaction vs. intrusive ideation
   c. Brief psychotic reaction vs. dissociation
   d. Dissociation vs. intrusive ideation
   e. State dependent learning sequela vs. personality disorder
   f. Acute transitory cognitive impairment vs. severe incapacitation
   g. Failure to detect suicidal or homicidal cues
   h. Lack of familiarity with guidelines for psychological triage (especially, predictors of posttraumatic stress disorder) and referral
   i. Major depression vs. acute dysphoria
   j. Failure to refer for mental health services, when indicated.

☐☐☐

Chapter Five

The Systems Perspective: Critical Incident Stress Management (CISM)

☐☐☐

Psychological intervention subsequent to crises and even mass disasters has historically been characterized by reactive, event-centered practices. The crisis intervention movement itself has been a movement often conceptualized as an event-driven process with little appreciation for the variability inherent in the temporal trajectory of the human response to mass disasters. Univariate, or limited scope, crisis intervention models originated from community mental health initiatives (Parad, 1966; Parad & Parad, 1968; Langsley, Machotka, & Flomenhaft, 1971; Decker & Stubblebine, 1972), grief counseling (Lindemann, 1944), and community psychiatry movements (Caplan, 1961, 1964), as well as the "forward psychiatry" initiatives of the great world wars (Salmon, 1919; Artiss, 1963; Kardiner and Spiegel, 1947). More recent recommendations, however, have called for crisis intervention and disaster mental health services to be delivered in an integrated multi-component format (Everly & Mitchell, 1999; Kaminsky, McCabe, Langlieb, & Everly, 2005; in press).

Resistence, Resilience, Recovery: The Johns Hokins Model

The Johns Hopkins Perspectives Model of Disaster Mental Health (Kaminsky, McCabe, Langlieb, & Everly, 2005; in press) employs a resistance, resilience, and recovery construct as a basic framework for organizing an integrative approach to disaster mental health. We shall briefly describe the fundamental characteristics of this outcome-driven approach, while mentioning psychological and sociological interventions that might be suited to enhance each.

Resistance

In the present context, the term "resistance" refers to the ability of an individual, group, organization, or entire population not to exhibit manifestations of clinical distress, impairment, or dysfunction that might otherwise be anticipated with critical incidents, terrorism, and even mass disasters. Resistance may be thought of as a form of psychological or behavioral immunity to distress and dysfunction.

Historically, this element of disaster mental health response was conspicuous in its absence. The notion of creating resistance represents a proactive step in emergency mental health. The introduction of this intervention to the pre-incident phase of the temporal continuum invites comparisons with the concepts of *psychological immunization* and *psychological body armor*.

Hardiness (Kobasa, Maddi, & Kahn, 1982) is believed to be an insulating factor against stressors. Hardiness is characterized by the belief in one's own self-efficacy, i.e., the ability to exert control over relevant life events; the tendency to see stressful events as "challenges" to be overcome; and a strong commitment and sense of purpose.

Thus, the first goal of the Johns Hopkins Perspectives Model of Disaster Mental Health would be to build resistance. Mechanisms by which hardiness-like resistance may be created include the following:

1. Perception of credible and competent leadership
2. Anticipatory guidance, setting appropriate expectations
3. Realistic training
4. Identification with a common purpose or goal
5. Identification with a higher ideal
6. Identification with a group; fostering of group identity
7. Fostering impact- and acute-phase task orientations
8. Stress management training
9. Provision of family support, as indicated

Resilience

In the present context, the term "resilience" refers to the ability of an individual, group, organization, or entire population, to rebound rapidly and effectively from psychological or behavioral disturbances associated with critical incidents, terrorism, or mass disasters.

The second goal of the Johns Hopkins Perspectives Model of Disaster Mental Health would be to enhance the resiliency of targeted personnel. Processes by which resilience may be enhanced include the following:

1. assessment of need
2. effective leadership

3. sustaining a credible, accurate information flow
4. stress management
5. sstablishment and utilization of social support networks
6. fostering an acute phase task orientation
7. implementation of "psychological first aid"
8. utilization of small group crisis intervention for naturally occurring cohorts and families
9. pastoral crisis intervention and chaplaincy services
10. psychological triage

Recovery

Finally, the term "recovery" refers to the ability of an individual, group, organization, or entire population to recover the ability to function adaptively — emotionally, mentally and behaviorally — in the wake of significant clinical distress, impairment, or dysfunction subsequent to a critical incident, terrorist event, or mass disaster. The final goal of the Johns Hopkins Perspectives Model of Disaster Mental Health would be to serve as a platform for facilitating access to continued support and clinical services.

Critical Incident Stress Management (CISM): Core Elements

One strategic system for the formulation and delivery of crisis and disaster mental health services which is consistent with the Johns Hopkins formulation of resilience is Critical Incident Stress Management (CISM; Everly & Mitchell, 1999).

The integrated and comprehensive multicomponent CISM system is depicted in Table 4.

Pre-event planning or "pre-incident preparation" occurs in the pre-crisis phase. The goals of pre-incident preparation are to set the appropriate expectancies for personnel as to the nature of the crisis and trauma risk factors they face. The corollary of this expectancy is to teach basic crisis coping skills in a proactive manner. As we enter the acute crisis phase we see the employment of various on-scene and peri-scene psychological support interventions.

Assessment refers to the active process wherein the actual need for intervention is assessed. Assessment may be performed upon individuals, small groups, and even large groups. The assumption that exposure to a traumatic event is the necessary and sufficient condition for active mental health intervention is a weak, if not false, assumption. Intervention should

Table 4
Summary of Commonly Used Crisis Intervention Tactics

INTERVENTION	TIMING	TARGET GROUP	POTENTIAL GOALS
Pre-event Planning/ Preparation	Pre-event	Anticipated target / victim population	Anticipatory guidance, foster resistance, resilience.
Assessment	Pre-intervention	Those directly & indirectly exposed	Determiniation of need for intervention.
Strategic planning	Pre-event & during event	Anticipated exposed and victim populations	Improve overall crisis response.
Individual Crisis Intervention (including "psychological first aid")	As needed	Individuals as needed	Assessment, screening, education, normalization, reduction of acute distress, triage, and facilitation of continued support.
Large Group Crisis Intervention * Demobilization	Shift disengagement, end of deployment	Emergency personnel	Decompression, ease transition, screening, triage education and meet basic needs.
* Respite center	Ongoing, large scale events	Emergency personnel, large groups	Respite, refreshment, screening, triage and support.
* Crisis Management Briefing (CMB) and large group "psychological first aid"	As needed	Heterogeneous large groups	Inform, control rumors, increase cohesion.
Small Group Crisis Intervention * Small Group Crisis Management Briefing (sCMB).	On-going and post-event; may be repeated as needed	Small groups seeking infomation / resources	Information, control rumors, reduce acute distress, increase cohesion, facilitate resilience, screening and triage.
* Defusing (and small group "psychological first aid")	On-going events and post-events (≤ 12 hours)	Small homogeneous groups	Stabilization, ventilation, reduce acute distress, screening, information, increase cohesion, and facilitate resilience

INTERVENTION	TIMING	TARGET GROUP	POTENTIAL GOALS
Small Group Crisis Intervention (continued)			
* Group debriefing (CISD, PD, NOVA MSD, CED, HERD)	Post - event; ~1 - 10 days for acute incidents, ~3 - 4 weeks post - disaster recovery phase	Small homogeneous groups with equal ventilation, trauma exposure (e.g., workgroups, emergency services, military)	Increase cohesion, information, normalization, red acute distress, facilitat resilience, screening and triage. Follow-up essential.
Family Crisis Intervention	Pre-event; as needed	Families	Wide range of interventions (e.g., pre-event preparation, individual crisis interventions, CMB, CISD or other group processes.)
Organizational / Community Intervention, Consultation	Pre-event; as needed or disaster	Organizations affected by trauma response.	Improve organizational preparedness and Leadership consultation.
Pastoral Crisis Intervention	As needed	Individuals, small groups, large groups, congregations, and communities who desire faith - based presence / crisis intervention	Faith - based support
Follow - up referral	As needed	Intervention recipients and exposed indivduals	Assure continuity of care

be predicated upon a demonstrated behavioral need, or a request for intervention.

Strategic planning. Mental health intervention in the wake of traumatic events and mass disasters requires an integrated, multi-component application system. Intervention must be flexible and fluid depending upon changing needs. In order to accomplish such a goal, strategic planning is essential. Table 2 (in Chapter 4) can actually assist in such planning by matching the interventions to the target groups and desired outcome.

Individual crisis support can be applied on-scene during a crisis event or at anytime after such an event. The key factor here is that this intervention is done one-on-one, that is, one individual support person assisting one (or perhaps two) individual(s) in crisis. Individual psychological first aid (PFA) would be an applicable intervention within this genre (Everly & Flynn, 2005).

*Demobilizations, Respite Centers, and Crisis Management Briefing*s are large group interventions. *Demobilizations* are used at mass disaster venues to assist rescue and disaster response personnel to decompress and transition from the disaster site to home or work. Upon occasion, the demobilization will be used with primary victims. The demobilization consists of a process wherein individuals, once disengaged from the crisis venue, receive refreshments and an informational briefing about stress, trauma, and coping techniques. It usually takes about 20 - 30 minutes. Informational handouts are distributed.

Respite centers are similar to demobilizations, but are used at mass disasters on an ongoing basis as opposed to the termination of a shift or callout.

The *crisis management briefing* (CMB) is a technique where a large group of individuals is brought together for a briefing, i.e., the conveyance of information pertaining to the crisis event. In a school setting, for example, an entire grade may be aggregated in the auditorium to receive information on a crisis that has effected the student body. Once the facts surrounding the event are communicated, a brief "teaching" session is conducted wherein the specific psychological issues are addresses in lecture-like format. For example, generic information on suicide or grief might be communicated. Finally, local school and community resources are introduced to serve as follow-up resources for those who have further concerns. The same technique can be used in business and industry with organizational workgroups.

Defusings, small group crisis management briefings, and Critical Incident Stress Debriefings are intended for small groups. *Defusings* may be done at the crisis venue after disengagement from the crisis activity or anywhere in the post-crisis phase within 12 hours after a crisis. Defusings are 20 - 45 minute interactive group discussions of the crisis event designed to reduce acute stress and tension levels. There are conducted with small homogeneous groups.

Small group crisis management briefings (sCMB) are also conducted with small groups. There are informational in nature. Group homogeneity is not essential.

Critical incident Stress Debriefings (CISD) are also interactive group discussions of a crisis or traumatic event. However, they are more detailed and more structured than the defusing. The CISD consists of seven phases.

It is highly interactive as opposed to informational, such as the briefing. The goal is to achieve a sense of psychological closure with regard to the crisis event. As a result, the CISD is usually most effective if done two to 10 days after the event has concluded. In mass disaster situations, they may be effectively done three to four weeks after the disaster. They usually take one to three hours to complete. There are numerous variations of the CISD (HERD, NOVA, CED, PD, etc.).

Family Interventions and Organizational Interventions. Any person who belongs to a family unit and experiences a crisis brings the effects of the crisis home to the other family members in both direct and indirect ways. Some form of post-incident family, or "significant other" support is highly encouraged. A specialized family debriefing may even be utilized. Religious/ spiritual support is often provided within such services, but can obviously be applied wherever they are best received.

Organizations can be victims of violence, crisis, and disaster, as well. It is important that organizations have some form of crisis and disaster plan. While many organizations now have crisis or disaster plans, they often lack sufficient attention to the human element from a psychological perspective.

Pastoral Crisis Intervention Services. Spiritual or religious themes are often present in trauma and disaster. It seems important to have available crisis intervention resources that can address such needs. The purpose of this volume is to facilitate that process.

Follow-up Referral. One of the great values of CISM services is that they serve as a feeder system, or facilitator, for the utilization of employee assistance programs and other mental health assessment and treatment services. Without crisis support services such as these it is likely that many individuals, who need such follow-up care, would simply not obtain it.

The development of an integrated, multi-component approach to crisis and disaster mental health is not without precedent. The parallel of psychotherapy seems appropriate to review. Historically, the field of psychotherapy appeared to evolve through three distinct phases: the univariate, the eclectic, and the integrative. The early years of psychotherapy were characterized by the practice of a multitude of diverse, univariate psychotherapeutic practices based upon singular theoretical orientations of psychopathology and healing, such as behavior therapy, person-centered psychotherapy, and psychoanalysis, to name a few. Rivalry among psychotherapeutic orientations has a long and undistinguished history.

Later, there seemed to be recognition that the aforementioned schools and their psychotherapeutic practices could co-exist, but not coincidentally. The eclectic phase saw the implementation of a singular intervention chosen from a collection of possible interventions, based upon a multitude of theoretical mechanisms of action. The selection of the intervention mechanism was based upon the clinician's assessment as to which intervention best suited the needs of the patient at that point in time.

Finally, the integrative approach to psychotherapy emerged. Integrative psychotherapy may be thought of as the implementation of an integrated array of psychotherapeutic interventions concurrently combined and catalytically sequenced in such a manner as to best respond to the unique needs, or "idiographic heterogeneity," of a given patient or group of patients. According to Millon, Grossman, Meagher, Millon, and Everly (1999), "The palette of methods and techniques available to the therapist must be commensurate with the idiographic heterogeneity of the patient for whom the methods and techniques are intended" (1999, p. 145).

The field of disaster mental health has evolved in a remarkably parallel fashion, progressing from univariate, to eclectic, to an integrative approach. Indeed, an integrative model for the multi-component approach to critical incident stress management has been previously described (Everly & Mitchell, 1999; Flannery & Everly, 2004; Everly & Langlieb, 2003).

Building upon those historical foundations, we see an integrative approach to disaster mental health, both strategically and tactically, as an integrated multi-faceted system incorporating a full continuum of care. Such an approach is consistent with Millon's concepts of potentiating pairings (using interacting combinations of interventions to achieve an enhancing clinical effect), catalytic sequences (sequentially combining tactical interventions in their most clinically useful ways), and polythetic selection (selecting the tactical interventions based on the specific needs of each situation). The various combinations and permutations that are actually utilized will be determined by the unique demands of each critical incident or disaster, and the unique demands of each target population, as they uniquely arise.

□□□

Chapter Six

Pastoral Crisis Intervention and the "10 Commandments" of Responding to Terrorism

With Cherie Castellano
(University of Medicine and Dentistry of New Jersey)

☐☐☐

The Evil Genie Unleashed

In 1992 Walt Disney Studios released an animated movie entitled *Aladdin*. It was to become a Disney "classic," entertaining millions. It was the story of a man who had discovered a genie in a bottle, a genie that would grant him three wishes. The promotional tagline for the movie was actually, "Imagine if you had three wishes, three hopes, three dreams and they all could come true."

The Disney movie *Aladdin* was actually based upon an Arabian fable translated in the mid-1800s by Sir Richard F. Burton and called *Tales of the Arabian Nights*. But Burton's description of the genie was somewhat different than that created by Disney. Burton described the genie as an ancient and powerful evil force who was inclined to destroy those who released him from the bottle. Only through the calm, strength, and wisdom shown by those who discovered him, was the genie safely returned to his bottle.

At 8:15 on the morning of August 6, 1945, an atomic bomb named "Little Boy" was dropped on Hiroshima, Japan, by a Boeing B-29 bomber, the Enola Gay. This detonation over Hiroshima created an atomic holocaust. The devastation was so complete, so profound that many feared that we had unleashed a powerful "atomic genie," a genie that was so powerful it could spell the end of humanity as we know it. In the August 19, 1946, issue of *Life* magazine, Admiral William H. P. Blandy called the atomic bomb "a poison weapon."

The Genie and the Cuban Missile Crisis

In the wake of Hiroshima, there was talk of trying to put the "genie" back into the bottle, as Sir Richard F. Burton's hero had done. But there was no going back. Once the genie was unleashed, this ancient and powerful force was not to be restrained by any physical force known to the human race. In fact, we further researched and expanded its destructive capabilities. But realistically, the only force that serves to hold this genie in restraint is the human will, the conscious decision not to unleash the awesome powers of the atomic genie in war. This fact was demonstrated during the 14 days of October, 1962, when the Soviet Union and the United States stood on the brink of thermonuclear war. It was Soviet Chairman Nikita Khrushchev's conscious decision not to risk a nuclear holocaust and to withdraw his missiles from Cuba that averted an unthinkable horror. As Secretary of State Dean Rusk stated on December 8, 1962, "We were eyeball to eyeball and the other fellow blinked." Khrushchev's psychological restraint would ultimately allow the realization of historical milestones such as *detente*, the demise of the Berlin Wall, and the collapse of Communism in much of the world.

Terrorism and the Genie

Terrorism represents a form of "evil genie," an ancient and powerful force capable of remarkable devastation. Indeed, it may be a "poison weapon" as Admiral Blandy remarked. *Terrorism* may be defined as the illegal, immoral use, or threatened use of force, designed to create conditions of fear, helplessness, and demoralization as a coercive or punitive force. More importantly, terrorism is psychological warfare, the goal of which is to demoralize the target group to the point that it surrenders to the will of the terrorists. From a planning perspective, it is important to see terrorism as a strategic weapon that targets the sources of a nation's military, economic, and political power...the civilian population! Terrorism targets:

- your sense of safety ("I'm affraid to do what I normally do.")
- your sense of justice and fair play ("That's not right, fair...")
- your sense of order, meaning ("It doesn't make sense...How could anyone do such a thing?")

Death and destruction are merely means to an end, they are not ends unto themselves. Terrorism seeks to create "psychological casualties," ie, individuals who become impaired as a result of the terrorism. The adverse impact of terrorism may, therefore, be estimated not just in terms of physical destruction, but in terms of psychological "toxicity." Factors that may serve to increase psychological toxicity might include:

1. unpredictable pattern of attacks,
2. ability to affect large numbers of victims,
3. intent to harm noncombatants, especially targeting women and children,
4. ease of weapon delivery,
5. delay and difficulty in assessing exposure, especially lethality,
6. long latency or incubation period, at least several days,
7. potential for contagion (physical or psychological), especially if it deters emergency response and/or treatment,
8. potential to scar and disable, rather than kill,
9. ability to overwhelm public health and other resources, while altering the accepted and preferential way of life,
10. motivation that is immune to rational, measured deterrence; willingness to use self-destruction as a weapon; all or nothing strategic thinking.

Terrorism and Total War

Total war is a concept first described by Karl von Clausewitz in a book entitled *Vom Kriege* (On War) published in 1832. The concept is simple...attack anything associated with the enemy...attack the sacred, attack the strategic sources of power, kill the innocent, do the unthinkable, demoralize until the enemy capitulates. The two points to be remembered here are that 1) terrorism may be fought as a form of total warfare, with no limitations, no boundaries; 2) total warfare may lead to an escalating spiral wherein "mutually assured destruction" is actually realized (especially in a war that is fought on religious grounds and martyrdom is a recognized virtue).

Psychological Counterterrorism: We Can Put the Genie Back into the Bottle

The overall goals of psychological counterterrorism are two-fold:

1. to reduce the likelihood that psychological terrorism will be used as a weapon; and
2. to bolster the psychological resistance and resilience of the targets of terrorism (military, emergency responders, and civilian).

First, in effect, we desire to achieve what the Sir Richard F. Burton's hero achieved…to put the genie back into the bottle. This cannot be achieved by approaching terrorism and terrorists on solely a tactical level using a military strike and counterstrike methodology. Rather a strategic response is necessary. We must target the source of terrorism, but this is not what you may think. We must target the psychological source of terrorism…the *motivation* to use terrorism as an agent for change.

It will be recalled that the only force that serves to hold the atomic genie in restraint is the human will, the conscious decision not to unleash the awesome powers of the atomic genie in war. This immutable reality applies to terrorism as well… the only force that serves to hold the genie of terrorism in restraint is the human will, the conscious decision not to unleash the destructive powers of terrorism. The most powerful of all approaches to reduce the motivation to use terrorism is a sociological one, one wherein justice exists and terrorism is unimaginable.

Secondly, bold new initiatives must be undertaken to increase the psychological and behavioral *resistance and resilience* of the military, emergency responders, and civilian populations. Resistance may be thought of as a psychological immunity to the effects of terrorism. Resiliency may be thought of as the ability to rebound from adversity. Winston Churchill, Franklin D. Roosevelt, John F. Kennedy, and Ronald Reagan all understood this. While some is known about each of these, much more research is needed.

Resiliency is fostered through understanding the adversary, regaining some control over your life, building networks for mutual support, and rediscovering some sense of meaning and purpose in life that has a future orientation, eg, identifying with something greater than yourself. In cases of loss, keeping in mind that the best way to honor those you have lost is to live well with a sense of purpose. It may be obvious by now that spiritual and religious interventions may be for some uniquely powerful in combating the unthinkable, the demoralizing, and even the use of total warfare. The pastoral crisis interventionist must have a working knowledge of the psychology of terrorism and psychological counterterrorism in order to be most effective. Consider the following:

"10 Commandments" for Building Stress Resilience in Response to Terrorism

1. "Know thyself"

Never lose sight of the fact that the terrorist act is designed to engender psychological instability, especially demoralization. It is essential that we identify our psychosocial strengths and harness them. It is also essential that we identify our psychosocial vulnerabilities and protect them.

2. **"Know thy enemy as you know thyself."** *(Sun Tzu)*

While it is essential to know oneself...strengths, weaknesses, normal reactions, more severe reactions...it is also essential to know the enemy and how the enemy will likely behave. Resources must be allocated to the analysis and prediction of the enemy's behavior.

3. **"And he shall lead them"**

"Crisis leadership" skills are a unique form of leadership seldom taught in traditional leadership classes. They are essential in building a comprehensive psychological counterterrorism arsenal. Crisis leadership aims to foster productivity while encouraging recognition of emotional and psychological implications of terrorist events.

4. **"It was then that I carried you..."**

Establish psychological support initiatives utilizing crisis intervention hotlines, outreach personnel, and crisis centers as needed. Given that the target of the terrorist is the mind, and that terrorism is psychological warfare, any resource directed to support psychological health may not only be seen as fostering health, but may be seen as fostering national defense. Finally, psychological first aid should be taught as readily as physical first aid in schools, in the workplace, and in public health and safety settings.

5. **"Honor thy family"**

For civilians, family is the first line of aid and support. For counterterrorism personnel, family is not only a source of support, but the family may inadvertently become a target for expressed frustrations. Town meetings, family support groups, printed materials and websites, spiritual activities and family counseling may be necessary on a regular or intermittent basis to provide support and strengthen that imperative resource.

6. "Be Your Brother's Keeper"

Foster the creation of organizational and community support networks. Provide relevant and timely information. Information is power. Rumors can be destructive to the workforce, family, and community.

7. "Foster the familiar."

Re-establish normal communication, transportation, economic, educational, and work schedules as soon as possible. There is safety in the familiar.

8. "Honor the living and the dead"

Understand and utilize the power of symbols, such as the cross at Ground Zero, as a means of reestablishing cohesion. Flags, signs, patriotic slogans can create a universal experience and connection among units, agencies and civilians.

9. "Start Anew"

At times, there will be a need to move an organization, community, or nation ahead after some catastrophic experience by creating a new epoch or era of rebirth... "a new beginning." Foster a focus upon the future and those things greater than yourself, such as religion, spirituality, national pride, and building a better world for our children.

10. "That which does not kill me makes me stronger" (Nietzsche)

Positive outcomes and growth can occur for some who are exposed to a terrorist event. Adversity may also be an opportunity to experience growth in personal awareness, spirituality and family resolutions.

As we learned from the attack on Pearl Harbor and the relentless bombing of London, during the "Battle of Britain," acts designed to demoralize and defeat can actually serve to strengthen. With the same calm, strength, and wisdom that returned the evil genie in the Arabian fables to his bottle, we can defeat terrorism...these are the principles of psychological counterterrorism.

Chapter Seven

A Word of Caution in the Application of Pastoral Crisis Intervention

□□□

Recently, the endeavor of providing early psychological intervention has been re-examined. Some have even called for an end to early intervention due to concern over potential iatrogenic harm as a result of crisis intervention, especially the ill-defined "psychological debriefing." Indeed, the term "debriefing," albeit poorly defined to the point of having lost any valuable denotative quality (NIMH, 2002), has come to inappropriately symbolize virtually all early psychological intervention. It now serves as a veritable "lightning rod" for the debate on early psychological intervention. Nevertheless, concern over possible harm resulting from crisis intervention is a valid concern.

The primary scientific foundation for the recent criticisms of early crisis intervention, especially "debriefing," can be found in the Cochrane Library's Cochrane Reviews. Citing as evidence the results of the Cochrane Library Review of RCTs (Rose, Bisson, & Wessely, 2002; Wessely, Rose, & Bisson, 1998) and selected derivative reviews (Litz, Gray, Bryant, & Adler, 2002; van Emmerick, Kamahis, Hulsbosch, & Emmelkamp, 2002), some have reached the conclusion that early psychological intervention (especially "debriefing") is ineffectual and may cause harm to some. A few individuals have even suggested that early intervention after disasters and mass violence should be discontinued in deference to waiting 30 days posttrauma and prescribing 4-12 sessions of cognitive behavioral therapy (CBT), although most authorities agree on the value of some form of "psychological first aid."

Such conclusions based upon the Cochrane Review, its derivatives, or selected combinations of constituent studies may not be warranted, however. In point of fact, most of the constituency of Cochrane investigations represent "single session counseling with medical patients" and are in no way consistent with the principles, nor the practice, of crisis intervention in community or mass disaster settings (Wessely & Deahl, 2003). As such, they fail to serve as a valid comparison group from which generalizations may be made to survivors of mass disasters or even emergency services personnel (Wessely & Deahl, 2003). Thus, those calling for the cessation of early intervention who use the Cochrane Review as the basis for their recommendation have extrapolated beyond the recommendations of even the Cochrane authors themselves. The authors of the Cochrane Review of psychological debriefing (Rose, Bisson, & Wessely, 2002), although calling for a cessation of "compulsory debriefings pending further evidence" (p. 10) have themselves concluded, *"We are unable to comment on the use of group debriefing, nor the use of debriefing after mass traumas" (p.10).*

Even Psychotherapy May Be Harmful

The field of psychotherapy preceded the formal development of the field of crisis intervention. There may be some useful lessons therein. As the field of psychotherapy developed, it should be noted that concern was expressed regarding potential adverse iatrogenesis. Indeed, subsequent research revealed that while many patients are helped by psychotherapy, some are not, and some are even harmed by participation in psychotherapy.

There can be little disagreement with the assertion that psychotherapy can lead to negative outcomes. More specifically, Smith, Glass, and Miller (1980) in their meta-analytic review of more than 400 psychotherapy outcome studies found that about 9% of the reported effect was negative. Shapiro and Shapiro (1982), in an analysis of more than 1800 effect sizes, found that 11% were negative and 30% were null! Mohr (1995) compiled a review of more than 40 psychotherapy investigations, all of which identified deterioration as a result of psychotherapy. Lambert (2003), in his most recent analysis of psychotherapy effectiveness, states, "Despite the overall positive findings, a portion of patients who enter treatment are worse off when they leave treatment than when they entered" (p. 4). He estimates that about 5-10% of patients "deteriorate during treatment," while another 15-25% show no measured benefit. The notion of negative outcome as a result of psychotherapy is not a new revelation as Strupp, Hadley, and Gomes-Schwartz (1977), in their text *Psychotherapy for Better or Worse*, listed more than 40 studies from 1950 to 1972 alone that reported negative outcome.

The field of traditional psychotherapy is not the only mental health intervention that possesses the potential for iatrogenic adversity. In their text *"Helping the Helpers Not to Harm: Iatrogenic Damage and Community Mental Health,"* Caplan and Caplan (2001) skillfully point out the risks associated with community mental health initiatives.

Crisis Intervention: A Cautionary Note

Clearly, however, in light of research suggesting that crisis intervention can exert positive effects, efforts should be directed toward identifying mechanisms of therapeutic effect, potential sources of adverse iatrogenesis, and compensatory strategies developed to respond to the latter. It would seem that such is a superior course as opposed to adopting reductionistic binary thinking wherein we view, and therefore subsequently judge, crisis intervention to be "all good" or "all bad." It seems that we would want to avoid a condition wherein we "throw the baby out with the bathwater."

A review of relevant literature reveals potential "risk factors" of significance associated with crisis intervention. Those risk factors are listed below with suggestions for mitigating those risks.

1. It is imperative that emergent intervention follow the basic principles and hierarchy of needs, i.e., meeting basic needs first. More specifically, needs for food, water, shelter, alleviation of pain, reunification with family members, and the provision of a sense of safety and security should all precede the utilization of psychologically-oriented crisis interventions.

2. As compulsory participation in crisis intervention is likely to be perceived negatively, participation in any psychologically-oriented crisis intervention activities should be voluntary, accompanied by some form of relevant informed consent when intervention goes beyond simple information or educational briefings.

3. Group crisis intervention poses a risk for iatrogenic harm if it introduces traumatogenetic material to group members who would not otherwise be exposed to such material. To reduce this risk, it is suggested that small crisis intervention groups be made up of naturally occurring cohorts and/or homogeneous groups with regard to trauma exposure and toxicity. The formation of small heterogeneous crisis intervention debriefings should not be endorsed.

4. It is hard to accept this notion of potential mass hysteria as a reason to "keep information from people for their own good." Nevertheless, it may be argued that the manner in which the information is presented may have a significant effect upon subsequent hysterical symptomatology. Such information should be presented as basic health education related information, designed to empower the recipients of such information to assume more, not less, control in responding to adversity, when such seems appropriate.

5. Research has clearly demonstrated the value of expressing the factual nature of stressful events in combinatin with their associated emotions (Koenig, 2004; Pennebaker & Beall, 1986). The notion of the value of cathartic ventilation has been challenged to the degree that concern has been expressed that cathartic ventilation may become a pathogenic abreactive process. To reduce this risk, it might be suggested that assessment and triage are essential elements of effective crisis intervention wherein psychologically vulnerable or brittle persons (highly aroused, morbidly depressed, highly guilt-ridden individuals, the intensely bereaved, dissociating individuals, those experiencing psychotic symptomatology, those physically injured or in pain) not be included in group crisis intervention; rather, they should be approached individually and more appropriate interventions should be utilized. Furthermore, whether individually or in groups, deep probing techniques, psychotherapeutic interpretation, and paradoxical intention should clearly be avoided.

6. Concern has been expressed that crisis intervention techniques should never consist of univariate stand-alone interventions. Rather, crisis intervention should consist of a phase sensitive, multi-variate intervention system. Consistent with the notion of integrative psychotherapy, crisis intervention should be integrative. Crisis intervention should be conceived of as a configurational system of strategies and tactics in which each intervention technique is selected not only for its efficacy in resolving singular clinical and pre-clinical features, but also for its contribution to the overall constellation of intervention procedures in their task of responding to the unique demands of any given circumstance (adapted from Millon, 2003).

7. Crisis intervention should not be conceived of as a substitute for more formal psychotherapeutic and/or psychiatric interventions. Crisis intervention should be seen as but one point on a continuum of care which certainly includes psychotherapy. The natural corollary of this conceptualization is that successful crisis intervention, similar to successful physical first aid, may actually consist of simply facilitating access to the next and more appropriate level of care.

8. Lastly, it is essential that those practicing psychological crisis intervention receive specialized training to do so (Dyregrov, 1999; Stapleton, 2004). Standard counseling and psychotherapy training will typically prove inadequate to respond effectively to mass disasters, large-scale violence, terrorism, and even well-circumscribed acute crises.

Can Pastoral Crisis Intervention Be Harmful?

As just described, while there are risks for adverse iatrogenesis associated with psychological crisis intervention, those risks may be mitigated. And because there are risks associated with psychological crisis intervention, it is logical to assume that there are risks associated with pastoral crisis intervention, as well. Table 3 (in Chapter 4) listed some of those risks. Here we review those of most concern. Furthermore, it may be possible to mitigate any such risks.

1. Undesired preaching – Perhaps one of the greatest concerns associated with any form of pastoral intervention is undesired preaching. In a crisis, individuals are uniquely vulnerable. Often this vulnerability manifests itself in heightened sensitivity. While preaching the gospel (of any given faith or religion) may have uniquely uplifting effects for those who are prepared to hear the message, unwanted preaching may engender anger, avoidance, resentment, and even shame. None of these reactions would be perceived as helpful in an acute crisis.

2. Attempts to "convert" – The attempt to convert the person in distress to a new religious or faith orientation must be resisted. Noting the aforementioned psychological vulnerability of the person in distress, more fundamental spiritual first aid interventions would seem indicated for those receptive to spiritual intervention, while more traditional psychological crisis intervention would seem more appropriate in cases where individuals are not receptive to a spiritual message.

3. Theological debates – The whole notion of provoking or even entering into a debate or argument of any kind with a person in acute distress seems beyond helpful. Not only does the person in distress possess a tendency to be overly sensitive to provocative cues, they possess a diminished ability to "hear" that which the speaker intends. Psychological alignment and the avoidance of conflict would seem a far better course of action.

4. Minimizing suffering as the "will of God" – Anything that is perceived as minimizing the significance of a loss or crisis or anything that appears to minimize the *validity* of one's acute distress is likely to engender resentment. Sometimes the best strategy is to admit that we are unsure as to the "why" of tragic events, while at the same time validating one's right to experience the distress. The pastoral crisis interventionist then participates in what is sometimes a difficult process of "attending to" and bearing witness to the distress of the

other through a process of active physical presence, active listening, and silence.

5. Using guilt/shame as motivation for change – The use of such tactics is controversial even outside of the context of pastoral crisis intervention. The use of such tactics within a crisis situation seems completely contraindicated.

Summary

This chapter has attempted to sensitize the reader and provide a cautionary note as to the risks for adverse iatrogenesis associated not only with psychological crisis intervention as we understand it, but also with pastoral crisis intervention.

While the yearning to assist another human being in distress is a truly noble instinct, it must be tempered with a sensitivity for the realization that even though help is offered it may not be well received. Further, even though help is offered, it has the potential to make any given situation worse . . . even though the intention is good, and even though that help may be offered in the name of God.

☐☐☐

Chapter Eight

A Disaster Spiritual Health Corps: Training the Faith Community to Respond to Terrorism and Catastrophe

O. Lee McCabe[1], Adrian Mosley[2], Howard S. Gwon[3], and Michael J. Kaminsky[4]

☐☐☐

This chapter describes the efforts of a partnership between several academic health centers and numerous faith-based organizations to develop a training program in disaster mental health for spiritual caregivers. The training curriculum integrated psychological first aid (PFA) content into a culturally-relevant spiritual framework. Nine pilot training sessions were conducted with 500 members of faith communities throughout Baltimore city and suburbs. Preliminary evaluation data indicate that trainees perceived the program as having significantly enhanced their knowledge of a model of crisis intervention that might be termed, "psycho-spiritual first aid," and increased their confidence in working with victims of trauma. The program is seen as having laid the foundation for an innovative, portable model of specialized early-responder training that can enhance the traditional roles of spiritual communities in public health emergencies.

The Role of Faith Communities in Disasters

It is well established that psychological casualties greatly outnumber physical casualties in following terrorist attacks and naturally occurring disasters (eg, Bradfield, 1989; Shalev & Soloman, 1996; Asukai, 1999; North et al., 1999; Boscarino et al., 2002; Galea et al., 2002; Schlenger et al., 2002; Ursano et al., 2003; and IOM, 2003). Furthermore, there are distinct subpopulations within the general population of disaster victims that are more at risk than others for developing acute and chronic post-trauma problems; these include urban minorities of low socioeconomic status whose vulnerability is often accentuated by chronic medical problems, severe mental illness, and substance use conditions (Smith et al., 1990; Lima et al., 1991; IOM, 2003; Pole et al., 2005).

Historically, faith-based organizations (FBOs) have been responsive in the aftermath of community disasters by providing tangible material resources, such as food, clothing, shelter, equipment, supplies, etc., as well as human services, such as death notification, prayer leadership, and general fellowship (Smith, 1978; Bradfield, Wylie, and Echterling, 1989). However, FBOs rarely are incorporated into formal preparedness and response operations of government (Koenig, 2006), nor are they fully recognized for their potential to provide effective emotional support for people with personal problems, in general (Verhoff, Kuhlka, and Couvan, 1981), or with trauma-induced symptoms following terrorist attacks or natural disasters (Chinicci, 1985), in particular. The failure to officially recognize the spiritual community as a vital, indigenous resource for frontline psychological interventions for trauma, and to foster the important community attributes of disaster resilience, resilience and recovery (Kaminsky, McCabe, Langlieb, & Everly (2006) is inconsistent with survey data documenting that clergy routinely devote 15% of their (50 hour) work week counseling members of their congregations (Weaver, 1995 quoted in Koenig, 2006) and that the psychiatric disorders impelling congregants to seek help from their pastors are as severe as those treated by mental health professionals (Larson, 1988).

The premise of the program to be described is that the faith community is an especially valuable resource that can fit logically into local, state, and federal emergency response systems. However, if such a role is to be actualized, a number of challenges must be successfully addressed. These include creating the necessary collaborations among key stakeholders to develop appropriate training opportunities to teach crisis intervention knowledge and skills to clergy; establishing a trainee database/registry of prospective responders; and developing government/community linkages for call-up and deployment.

The authors addressed the above challenges by a) creating a partnership between several academic health centers and local faith communities to develop a training curriculum integrating disaster mental health content — specifically, "psychological first aid" (PFA; Everly and Flynn, 2005; Everly and Parker, 2006) with the values, perspectives, and communication styles of selected spiritual communities; b) tailoring the curriculum to fit the religious (*Christian*) and cultural characteristics of poor, urban African-American and non-English speaking Latino residents; c) collecting data to demonstrate participants' post-training perception of increased self-efficacy as a provider of disaster ministry; and d) establishing the administrative scaffolding upon which to build a volunteer trainee database and deployment infrastructure.

A Funding Opportunity to Expand the Role of the Faith Community in Disasters

The opportunity to pursue these initiatives came in the form of a grant program, administered by the Office of Preparedness and Response of the Maryland Department of Health and Mental Hygiene (MD-DHMH), the original source of funding being the Special Projects grant program for hospital preparedness, sponsored by the Health Resources and Services administration (HRSA) of the US Department of Health and Human Services. The grant application was developed by the Johns Hopkins Department of Psychiatry and Behavioral Sciences on behalf of the Johns Hopkins Hospital and other partnering organizations [see 'Partnership Entities...etc' below].

The Progam

Program Assumptions and Tasks

The logic of the grant application was that FBOs are ideal venues to support self- and other-referred individuals seeking trauma-related services of the kind needed following human- or naturally-caused community crises, particularly when a network of clergy has been trained in crisis/disaster mental health principles and interventions. To confirm this premise, however, the authors had to address multiple program design and implementation challenges in the brief period of time intrinsic to the HRSA (annual) grant cycle. Representative of these tasks were activities related to: establishing and nurturing institution/community partnerships; articulating the mission and vision; identifying objectives; managing day-to-day operations; designing and developing the curriculum; scheduling and conducting training sessions; and evaluating the program. These tasks were successfully accomplished and are described below.

Partnership Entities and Roles

Implementation of the project required coordination among numerous partners inside and outside the Johns Hopkins Medical Institutions. The intra-Hopkins participants included:

- The Johns Hopkins Office of Behavioral Health Care (JH-OBHC): JH-OBHC, in the Department of Psychiatry and Behavioral Sciences of the Johns Hopkins University School of Medicine, prepared the grant application and provided oversight of the post-award project implementation. The lead author (OLM) is the director of JH-OBHC, and was the Principal Investigator (PI) of the project.

- The Johns Hopkins Hospital (JHH): JHH, the first teaching hospital in North America, is a 1000+-bed, urban-based hospital with a long-standing commitment to the residents of East Baltimore, and was the formal recipient of the grant award. JHH sub-contracted the day-to-day management of the grant to JH-OBHC.

- The Johns Hopkins Office of Community Health (JH-OCH): JH-OCH was created in 1991 to facilitate the formation of community-academic partnerships to promote the health of citizens in the local community. The second author (AM) is the Administrator of JH-OCH and served the role of Project Coordinator.

- The Johns Hopkins Hospital Office of Pastoral Care (JH-OPC): The Acting Director of JH-OPC provided significant input to the "disaster ministry" component of the training curriculum.

- Office of Emergency Management (OEM), The Johns Hopkins Hospital: JH-OEM is responsible for all policies and procedures related to emergencies that might have a negative impact on hospital patients, staff, students, et al.

- Center for Public Health Preparedness, The Johns Hopkins Bloomberg School of Public Health (JH-CPHP): JH-CPHP is funded by a five-year grant from the Centers for Disease Control (CDC) and provides a diverse array of preparedness trainings in the mid-Atlantic region, with teaching formats customized to a variety of adult learning styles. Its role in the project was to provide general advice on project implementation, including valuable input on culturally-appropriate curriculum content.

The external community partners were:
- Archdiocese of Baltimore - Office of Hispanic Ministry: The Hispanic Ministry was established in 1963 to meet the health and psychosocial needs of Baltimore City's growing Latino population, often disenfranchised by language barriers, socio-economic hardship, and cultural differences. It's role in the project was to provide advice on all matters related to the local Hispanic population and clergy, and to provide assistance with the English-to-Spanish translation of the curriculum.

- Clergy United for Renewal in East Baltimore (CURE): CURE, an ecumenical organization of clergy established in 1987, has a long history of collaboration with Johns Hopkins Medical Institutions. Through its member churches and clergy, CURE has worked to bring culturally appropriate health messages to East Baltimore's African-American church congregations and neighborhoods. The role of CURE in the instant project was to assist with outreach (clergy recruitment) to the east Baltimore spiritual community and with curriculum development. It's co-founder/immediate past-president also functioned as a trainer.

- Institute for Mental Health Ministry, Inc: The Institute was established in 2001 and provides a full range of clinical services, within the framework of a bio-psycho-spiritual model, to those seeking spiritually sensitive and inclusive treatment. The founder and director of the Institute is a board-certified psychiatrist who is also an ordained minister. He contributed content to the curriculum and conducted training sessions.

- University of Maryland Department of Psychiatry and Behavioral Sciences (UM-DoP): UM-DoP is well-known for serving the behavioral health needs of Baltimore residents, especially those in the western neighborhoods of the Baltimore City. UM-DoP was responsible for outreach to FOBs in the western neighborhoods of Baltimore City (while Johns Hopkins was responsible for outreach to the east Baltimore community).

A note on the Partnership Philosophy - Beginning at the grant application stage, the authors emphasized the importance of creating a cohesive, enduring academic-faith alliance. To accomplish this goal, an explicit "partnership philosophy" was articulated that recognized the following principles:

- Participants function in distinct cultures, and thus need to be committed to developing an environment that is mutually supportive of other partner needs;
- The principles of trust, respect, communication, flexibility, and mutual benefit are critical to the success of the partnership; and
- Collaborators are committed to sharing resources, and to developing compatible goals, realistic plans, clear objectives, specified tasks, and shared credit among partners.

Boards, Committees, and Workgroups

The project was implemented through a Partnership Steering Committee, a Curriculum Development Committee, and a Community Advisory Board. The Steering Committee was comprised of one representative from each of the partnering entities and the PI who chaired the committee. The

Steering Committee met monthly for the first two months and bi-monthly for the duration of the project; this group made key decisions regarding strategies and tactics for project implementation. The Curriculum Committee was composed of at least one representative from all partnering organizations; it met on a weekly basis, and its members designed all of the content of the PPT slide presentation and Resource ('Tool') Kit. The Steering Committee and the Curriculum Committee were empowered to charter ad hoc committees and workgroups, as needed. Members of the Advisory Board, all of whom were leaders in the faith community, were selected by the director of JH-OCH. The advisory board met on a monthly schedule, provided helpful input on operationalizing the "partnership philosophy," and accepted accountability for outreach to members of their respective congregations to assure the recruitment of prospective trainees.

Program Vision and Mission

Vision - The long-term vision for the program was for the state of Maryland to formally recognize specially-trained leaders and congregations in the faith community as a vital resource in its continuum of frontline disaster workforce responders.

Mission - The near-term mission was to begin enhancing the capacity of clergy and lay leaders to respond to members of their communities who might need support during and following disasters of varying types and scope. The mission was to be accomplished through a training program designed by the partners. The project was originally conceived to benefit residents of the Greater Baltimore area, especially disadvantaged minority populations in the eastern and western neighborhoods of Baltimore City whose limited resources make them particularly vulnerable to disasters and large-scale community crises.

Program Objectives and Timetable

Award recipients under HRSA's Special Projects grant program must spend or obligate all funds by August 30th of the same year the award is given. Typically, notices of award are provided each year in the month of February. The project objectives during that compressed implementation period were as follows:

1. to develop a customized disaster preparedness [Microsoft Power Point (PPT)] curriculum with content that a) reflected the cultures of the clergy and the vulnerable populations with whom they work; b) possessed biological, psychological and spiritual components; c) functionally bridged the public health and clerical approaches to an all-

hazards mental health emergency response; and d) was compatible with state of Maryland's scope-of-practice statutes and related regulations;

2. to develop a disaster preparedness curriculum with knowledge-application and skill-building exercises that would encourage active involvement in training and promote the acquisition of competencies that would transfer to real-life contexts and circumstances;

3. to develop a disaster "tool kit" that provided for trainees a comprehensive collection of practical resources;

4. to develop a training manual to promote high fidelity replication of the model;

5. to complete the program with a minimum of 240 trained members of the faith community;

6. to develop a database of contact information on trained faith leaders that would be the foundation for a Volunteer Disaster Spiritual Health Corp Registry; and

7. to establish the foundation for a formal liaison entity between the FBOs and local and state disaster management agencies for the coordination and efficient deployment of clergy during and following public health crises.

The Training Curriculum: Format, Content, etc.

Format of Training Sessions - Training sessions were conducted using a professional CME/CEU format, ie, one-day in length (9:00 a.m. through 4:00 p.m.) with lunch and morning and afternoon refreshment breaks. Each session opened and closed with a prayer. Program evaluations were completed at the end of the day, following which a "commissioning" of participants was conducted and certificates of attendance distributed.

Trainers - All training sessions were conducted by teams composed of one mental health expert and one clergy member.

Content - The topics covered in the training, listed in the sequence in which they were presented, are as follows:

1. Stress Reactions of Mind, Body and Spirit: a) Acute Stress; b) Chronic/ Cumulative Stress and Burnout; c) PTSD;

2. Psychological First Aid and Crisis Intervention: a) Incident Command System; b) Individual Psychological First Aid; c) Large Group & Congregational Psychological First Aid;

3. Pastoral Care and Disaster Ministry: a) Fundamental Aspects of Disaster Ministry; b) Differentiating Traditional Pastoral Care and Disaster Pastoral Care; c) Responses: Pastoral and Prophetic;

4. Self Care and Practical Resources for Spiritual Caregivers: a) Recognizing and Preventing Burnout in Oneself; b) Self-Help Strategies; c) Disaster Planning and Resources for Families: Yours and Theirs.

A Note on Curriculum Customization - To personalize the effort and promote identification with curriculum content, the authors asked faith leaders to incorporate into the PPT slides their own selections of prayers, scriptural passages, religious images, church photographs, etc. Additionally, a Spanish language version of the PPT-slide program was created.

Evaluation

Interpretations of success in meeting the objectives of the program were derived from traditional *process data* (number of trainings, number of persons trained, etc.) and *outcome data* (trainee ratings via a structured evaluation form, administered immediately after each training session). The scope of evaluation items spanned perceptions of *overall program quality* and success of the program in meeting *specific learning objectives*. These variables were measured using a 5-point Likert scale. Additionally, there were structured opportunities for respondents to provide open-ended comments and recommendations about future training.

Process Evaluation

Trainers, Training Sessions, etc. - Collectively, a total of eight trainers were enlisted, viz, two doctoral-level psychologists with extensive disaster mental health experience and seven members of the clergy, including the aforementioned minister-psychiatrist. Five hundred members of the faith community were trained in a total of nine sessions. One Spanish- language training was delivered to 73 priests and laity from the local Hispanic faith community. Training sessions were delivered in diverse venues, ranging from auditoria of academic medical centers to small community churches, where attendees were seated in pews and trainers presented from a location in front of the altar.

Curriculum Development - The partners worked effectively in developing the 200-slide training program and tool-kit, the latter distributed to participants the morning of each training.

Database/Volunteer Registry - Basic demographic/contact data were collected on all trainees and incorporated into an Excel database, with a view to having this information as foundation for the eventual volunteer registry.

Call-Up/Deployment Mechanism - The JH-OEM will serve as the co-ordinating mechanism between the state of Maryland and the faith community to facilitate call-up and deployment of volunteers. The development of memoranda-of-understanding will be critical to this process.

Outcome Evaluation

A summary of the findings on trainee perceptions of the quality of the program is provided in Table 5.

The data indicate that the majority of participants considered the training either *very good* or *excellent* in overall quality and in accomplishing its learning objectives. The evaluation variable receiving the lowest score (73.6), ie, "quality of trainers: clergy members" was due to a relatively poor grading of one trainer's performance on one training day. [The occasion for this training was an annual conference of clinical pastoral counselors, all of whom possessed graduate education degrees. The training was conducted by an urban-based Baptist minister, filling in at the last minute for another scheduled trainer. Though well-meaning, the trainer periodically chastised attendees for what he viewed as the participants' unfamiliarity with parts of the Bible, and generally tended to embody the fire-and-brimstone style of teaching/preaching. [*It is instructive that the same trainer received exemplary ratings following a later training session with his own congregation, underscoring the importance of 'fit' between trainer/trainee characteristics.*] The evaluation process ended with the question, *Have you acquired any important information that you see being of help to you in the future as a leader in the clergy community?* The percentage of participants responding "Yes" was 98.4.

Conclusions

The authors' experience with this project has led to certain conclusions, the sharing of which is intended to benefit others who might seek to pursue similar initiatives in their own communities.

Notwithstanding the oft-observed tensions between large, urban-based teaching hospitals and their adjacent communities, the project demonstrated that, despite their disparate cultures, representatives from academic and faith organizations can enter into mutually-gratifying collaborations – in this

Table 5

Percent of Participants Rating Program as "Very Good" or "Excellent" in Its Effectiveness in Meeting Specific and General Objectives

General Objectives of Program Quality and Usefulness	Percent
Program Content	85.4
Likely Usefulness in the Event of a Disaster or Large Scale Critical Incident	84.3
Quality of Presentations: Disaster Mental Health Experts	91.8
Quality of Presentations: Clergy Members	73.6
Overall Program	89.1
Specific Learning Objectives	
Understanding the Principles of Providing Individual Psychological First Aid	85.5
Understanding the Principles of Providing Group/ Congregational Psychological First Aid	81.5
Gaining Awareness of Key Features of Disaster Ministry	85.9
Understanding Essentials of Disaster Planning and Self-Care Strategies for the Spiritual Caregivers	89.6
Understanding the Principles of Providing Individual Psychological First Aid	85.5

instance, to lay the foundation for a disaster spiritual health corps, the members of which have confidence in their ability to respond effectively to terrorist attacks, natural disasters, and other public health emergencies. Crucial to the success of these enterprises, it would seem, are leaders on each side of such partnerships who are fervent champions of and models for the collaboration.

Participants were enthusiastic in their expressions of interest in the information conveyed in the trainings. They were especially appreciative of the efforts to *integrate* the technical disaster mental health content with the spiritual; they routinely referred to training opportunity as "a gift from God." Although the prospects of large scale catastrophes were experienced as somewhat abstract or remote by some trainees, most participants had little difficulty finding immediate relevance in the training, as they routinely related the crisis intervention content to their everyday pastoral ministries.

Obviously, logical next steps in program advancement include the development of training curricula for members of other religious faiths. Based on specific trainee responses to open-ended questions in the evaluation form, there is also a need to create opportunities for: a) more advanced training in PFA; b) specialized training in loss/grief/bereavement support; c) development of concrete, practical, community disaster plans (and community empowerment, in general); and d) clarification of specific respondent roles under various disaster activation/deployment scenarios. [These initiatives are currently being pursued in a second MD-DHMH/HRSA grant].

Summing up, the above-described program would appear to be a practical and eminently portable model for actualizing the latent but typically unrealized potential for specialized disaster assistance, inherent in the already established relationship between vulnerable urban populations and faith leaders (and probably rural residents for whom access to health professionals, in general, and to disaster mental health experts, in particular, is limited). By implementing this model of training on a broader scale, the faith community could actualize its full potential of being an available, effective, and durable resource for victims of large-scale disasters, with benefits accruing both to individual recipients of direct psycho-spiritual services, and to managers of health care facilities who are struggling with the problem of how to cope with disaster-driven surges in service demand under various hazard scenarios, particularly when front-line clinical staffing may be significantly reduced.

Acknowledgment

The authors wish to express special thanks to:

—The Office of Preparedness and Response (Director, Al Romanosky, MD, PhD) of the Maryland Department of Health and Mental Hygiene for the support of this project by a Special Projects grant from the Bioterrorism Hospital Preparedness Program of the Health Resources and Services Administration's (HRSA);

—Drs. George S. Everly, Jr. and Jeffrey M. Lating for their assistance in developing substantive portions of the disaster mental health training curriculum; and

—All members of the academic-faith community partnership whose contributions of time, effort, and intellectual content have made this project a potentially promising model for widespread application to the societal problem of disaster-related human suffering.

(Footnotes)
[1]*Director, Behavioral Health Care and Associate Professor, Department of Psychiatry and Behavioral Sciences, The Johns Hopkins School of Medicine; Joint Appointment, Associate Professor, Department of*

Mental Health, The Johns Hopkins Bloomberg School of Public Health. [2]Administrator, Office of Community Health, The Johns Hopkins Health System. [3]Administrator, Office of Emergency Management, The Johns Hopkins Health System. [4] Vice Chair and Associate Professor, Department of Psychiatry and Behavioral Sciences, The Johns Hopkins School of Medicine.

PASTORAL CRISIS INTERVENTION - SPIRITUAL FIRST AID

☐☐☐

1) Stabilization & Introduction:
   a. Build trust relationship as an Ambassador of God
   b. Ministry of presence - message of acceptance and hope
   c. Serve as advocate or liaison to reduce stressors, if necessary/ possible.
2) Acknowledgement:
   a. Listen attentively, hearing the cry of person in crisis
   b. Listen for the concrete specifics of how the person feels "spiritual injury"
   c. Use empathic, reflective responses
3) Facilitate understanding:
   a. Validate the cry/injury
   b. Focus on the concrete specifics of how the person feels "spiritual injury"
4) Encourage adaptive spiritual coping
   a. Support person in exploring pereson's own coping, own answers
   b. Utilization of faith, its principles, & scriptures (if applicable) to promote healing
   c. Prayer, if appropriate; don't proselytize
   d. Delay any impulsive changes
   e. Your belief in/ encouragement of the person can make a difference
5) Referral/ Follow-up for continued dialogue, exploration, support

Appendix B

PASTORAL CRISIS INTERVENTION - THE THEODOLOTIC CRISIS

□□□

1. Stabilization & Introduction - Begin with... Ministry of Presence. Serve as advocate or liaison to reduce stressors, if necessary/ possible.

2. Acknowledgement - Let the person tell their "story." Be open to expressions of feelings (as opposed to actively encouraging catharsis). Be tolerant of silence. Listen carefully for the nature of the theodicy question.

3. Facilitate understanding - Offer empathic, reflective responses. Understand that questions of theodicy may be evidence of core faith disruption and may be the most common challenge faced.

4. Encourage adaptive coping during the acute theodolitic challenge
   a. The most common mistake that may be made is to try to "solve" the theodolitic dilemma in the moment of crisis.
   b. To begin, ask how the individual would desire to "understand" or "justify" the occurrence. That is, what "explanation" would be most comforting to them. Affirm such a conclusion as best you can (if you can) and support that interpretation, at least in the acute phase.
   c. In circumstances where there is no "most comforting" explanation, consider reliance upon faith (acceptance), while delaying the need to "understand" until referral for pastoral guidance/ counseling can be achieved. This approach is same as suicide intervention.

5. Referral for continued care, often pastoral counseling.

Appendix C

PASTORAL CRISIS INTERVENTION - THE SUICIDAL CRISIS (CCDR):
Clarify, Contradict, Delay, Refer

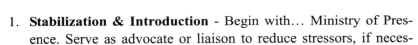

1. **Stabilization & Introduction** - Begin with… Ministry of Presence. Serve as advocate or liaison to reduce stressors, if necessary/ possible.

2. **Acknowledgement** - Let the person tell their "story." Be open to expressions of   feelings (as opposed to actively encouraging catharsis). Be tolerant of silence. Listen carefully for the roots of hopelessness.

3. **Facilitate understanding** - Offer empathic, reflective responses. Understand that issues of suicide are usually based in hopelessness, helplessness, and a sense that there is no future worth living. Secondary gain issues such as vengeance or financial factors cannot be ignored.

4. **Encourage acute coping** or, at least, willingness to delay the suicidal act (CCD):

    a. **Clarify** the intention.

      "Do you really want to die, or do you simply want to stop hurting?"

      "Do you really want to die, or do you simply want to live your life   differently?" A positive response to this question opens a host of non-lethal options.

    b. **Contradict** the notion that the intended outcome will be achieved.

      For example, suicide will create more problems than it solves. Suicide creates an adverse and undesired "ripple effect" affecting others.

    c. **Delay** (If the person seems intent upon suicide, consider arguing for a delay rather than trying to convince the person that suicide is wrong.) Point out that much may be gained and little lost by merely postponing the suicidal act. This tactic allows the person to obtain professional care that will be designed to ultimately eliminate the suicidal intention.

5. **Refer** - Facilitate access for evaluation and continued care. Actively assist in accessing continued care.

Appendix D

PASTORAL CRISIS INTERVENTION - GRIEF

☐☐☐

1. Stabilization & Introduction - Begin with... Ministry of Presence. Serve as advocate or liaison to reduce stressors, if necessary/ possible.
2. Acknowledgement - Be open to the telling (and retelling) of remembrances, family "stories,"etc. Be open to expressions of feelings (as opposed to actively encouraging catharsis). Be tolerant of silence.
3. Facilitate understanding - Offer empathic, reflective responses. Normalize, de-pathologize as appropriate. Prayer (if requested by the one who is grieving).
4. Encourage adaptive grieving and coping.
    a. Delay impulsive changes
    b. Transition from physical presence to something else (i.e. spirit, memory)
    c. Assist the individual in making some meaning out of the loss, if appropriate
    d. Assist individual in redefining how to live without the deceased ("how to live in the warmth of their memory")
    e. Teach basic stress management, if appropriate
5. Referral for continued care, if necessary. Always follow-up, when possible.

Appendix E

The Johns Hopkins Model of Psychological First Aid (RAPID-PFA)

□□□

Throughout this text, the term "psychological first aid" has been mentioned. Let us briefly review this important concept for those unfamiliar.

Most authorities agree that mass disasters leave in their wake a need for some form of acute mental health services. However, a review of current literature on crisis intervention and disaster mental health reveals differing points of view on the methods that should be employed (Raphael, 1986; NIMH, 2002). Nevertheless, there appears to be virtual universal endorsement, by relevant authorities, of the value of acute "psychological first aid" (American Psychiatric Association, 1954; DHHS, 2004; Raphael, 1986; NIMH, 2002; Institute of Medicine, 2003; WHO, 2003; DoD/ VAPTSD, Ritchie, et al., 2004; Friedman, et al., 2004).

In 1954, the American Psychiatric Association published the monograph entitled *Psychological First Aid in Community Disasters* (APA, 1954). That document therein defined and argued for the development of an acute mental health intervention, referred to as "psychological first aid" (PFA). This early exposition noted, "In all disasters, whether they result from the forces of nature or from enemy attack, the people involved are subjected to stresses of a severity and quality not generally encountered...It is vital for all disaster workers to have some familiarity with common patterns of reaction to unusual emotional stress and strain. These workers must also know the fundamental principles of coping most effectively with disturbed people. Although [these suggestions have] been stimulated by the current needs for civil defense against possible enemy action... These principles are essential for those who are to help the victims of floods, fires, tornadoes, and other natural catastrophes" (APA, 1954, p. 5). This seminal document delineated three important points:

1. The constituents of PFA consist of the ability to recognize common (and one might assume uncommon) reactions post disaster;

2. The constituents of PFA further consist of the fundamentals of coping; and

3. ALL disaster workers should be trained, not just mental health clinicians.

In the first truly integrative disaster mental health text, *When Disaster Strikes*, Beverley Raphael noted, "…in the first hours after a disaster, at least 25% of the population may be stunned and dazed, apathetic and wandering—suffering from the disaster syndrome—especially if impact has been sudden and totally devastating…At this point, psychological first aid and triage…are necessary…" (Raphael, 1986, p.257). More recently, the Institute of Medicine (2003) has written, "In the past decade, there has been a growing movement in the world to develop a concept similar to physical first aid for coping with stressful and traumatic events in life. This strategy has been known by a number of names but is most commonly referred to as psychological first aid (PFA). Essentially, PFA provides individuals with skills they can use in responding to psychological consequences of [disasters] in their own lives, as well as in the lives of their family, friends, and neighbors. As a community program, it can provide a well-organized community task to increase skills, knowledge, and effectiveness in maximizing health and resiliency" (IOM, 2003, p. 4-5). Finally, W. Walter Menninger (2002), based upon the work of Karen Horney, has stated that the goal of psychological first aid is to reduce feelings of isolation, helplessness, and powerlessness.

According to the Institute of Medicine (2003), "Psychological first aid is a group of skills identified to limit distress and negative health behaviors…"PFA generally includes education about normal psychological responses to stressful and traumatic events; skills in active listening; understanding the importance of maintaining physical health and normal sleep, nutrition, and rest; and understanding when to seek help from professional caregivers" (IOM, 2003, p.7).

The National Institute of Mental Health document, *Mental Health and Mass Violence* (2002), has enumerated the functions of psychological first aid as including the need to…

"Protect survivors from further harm,
Reduce physiological arousal,
Mobilize support for those who are most distressed,
Keep families together and facilitate reunions with loved ones,
Provide information and foster communication and education,
Use effective risk communication techniques" (p. 13).

The U. S. Department of Health and Human Services (DHHS, 2004) has compiled a list of "immediate mental health interventions." Within that list resides "psychological first aid." The components of psychological first aid include providing comfort, addressing immediate physical needs, supporting practical tasks, providing anticipatory information, listening and validating feeling, linking survivors to social support, normalizing stress reactions, and finally, reinforcing positive coping mechanisms.

Within the context of this volume, we define psychological first aid (PFA) as *"a supportive and compassionate presence designed to reduce acute psychological distress and/or facilitate continued support, if necessary."* PFA may be used in a wide variety of circumstances including the stressors of daily life, in family problems, in medical emergencies, in cases of loss and grief, and even in mass disasters. While the World Health Organization (2003) and the National Institute of Mental Health (2002) recognize the importance, and recommend the practice, of psychological first aid, there currently exist few, practical guidelines on how it may be implemented.

At the Johns Hopkins' Center for Public Health Preparedness (CPHP), under the direction of Dr. Jon Links, we sought to provide a practical structure for the application of psychological first aid. George S. Everly, Jr., PhD and Cindy L. Parker, MD, MPH developed the following set of guidelines for the practice of psychological first aid. These guidelines have been implemented as studies on content validity and clinical utility are currently underway with the assistance of Natalie Semon and Dan Barnett, MD, MPH.

Psychological first aid (PFA) may be operationally defined as consisting of the following functions:

Johns Hopkins' CPHP Model of Psychological First Aid (RAPID-PFA)

I. Reflective listening
II. Assessment
    A. Basic needs
    B. For triage
III. Prioritize benign vs. malignant stress reactions
IV. Intervention to manage stress and instill hope
    A. Acute cognitive refocusing/ re-orienting
    B. Deep breathing
    C. Cognitive reframing
        1. correction of errors in fact
        2. disputing illogical thinking
        3. challenging catastrophic thinking
        4. finding something positive, hidden benefit
    D. Instillation of a future orientation
    E. Delay in making any life-altering decisions/ changes
    F. Cautions
V. Discharge or facilitate access to continued care

Resources

□□□

American Red Cross (2001). *The ripple effect.* Alexandria, VA: Author.

American Psychiatric Association (1980). *Diagnostic and statistical manual of mental disorders,* Third Ed. Washington, DC: APA Press.

Artiss, K. (1963). Human behavior under stress: From combat to social psychiatry. *Military Medicine, 128,* 1011-1015.

Asukai, N. (1999). Mental health effects following man-made toxic disasters: The sarin attack and arsenic poisoning case. Presented at the 11ᵗʰ Congress of World Association for Disaster and Emergency Medicine. Osaka, Japan.

Bachman, R., (1994, July 6) Violence and theft in the workplace. *Crime data brief: National crime victimization survey.* Washington, DC: U.S. Department of Justice.

Barry, S. (2003). Pastoral counseling in the military. In R. Wicks, R. Parsons, & D Capps (Eds). *Clinical handbook of pastoral counseling,* Vol. III (pp.7-16). NY: Paulist Press.

Beaton, R., Murphy, S. & Corneil, W (1996, September). *Prevalence of posttraumatic stress disorder symptomatology in professional urban fire fighters in two countries.* Paper presented to the International Congress of Occupational Health, Stockholm, Sweden.

Bordow, S. & Porritt, D. (1979). An experimental evaluation of crisis intervention. *Social Science and Medicine,* 13, 251-256.

Boscarino, J.A., Adams, R.E., & Figley, C.R. (2005). A prospective cohort study of the effectiveness of employer-sponsored crisis interventions after a major disaster. *International Journal of Emergency Mental Health,* 7, 9-22.

Boscarino, J.A., Adams, R.E., Foa, E.B., & Landrigan, P.J. (2006). A propensity score analysis of brief worksite crisis interventions after the World Trade Center disaster: implications for intervention and research. *Medical Care,* 44(5):454-62.

Boscarino, J.A., Galea, S., Ahern, J., Resnick, H., & Vlahov, D. (2002). Utilization of mental health services following the September 11ᵗʰ terrorist attacks in Manhattan, New York City. *International Journal of Emergency Mental Health, 4,* 143-155.

Bowlby, J. (1969). *Attachment.* NY: Basic Books.

Bradfield, C., Wylie, M.L., & Echterling, L.G. (1989). After the flood: The response of ministers to natural disaster. *Sociological Analysis*, *49*, 397-407.

Brende, J.O. (1991). *Post-traumatic symptoms and trauma recovery in the Bible*. Columbus, GA: Trauma Recovery.

Breslau, N., Kessler, R., Chilcoat, H., Schultz, L., Davis, G., & Andreski, P. (1998). Trauma and posttraumatic stress disorder in the community. *Archives of General Psychiatry, 55*, 626-633.

Buckley, T.C., Blanchard, E., & Hickling, E. (1996) A prospective examination of delayed onset PTSD secondary to motor vehicle accidents. *Journal of Abnormal Psychology*, *105*, 617-625.

Bunn, T. & Clarke, A. (1979). Crisis intervention. *British Journal of Medical Psychology*, *52*, 191-195.

Campfield, K. & Hills, A. (2001). Effect of timing of Critical Incident Stress Debriefing (CISD) on posttraumatic symptoms. *Journal of Traumatic Stress*, 14, 327-340.

Caplan, G. (1961). *An approach to community mental health*. NY: Grune and Stratton.

Caplan, G. (1964). *Principles of preventive psychiatry*. NY: Basic Books.

Caplan, R. & Caplan, G. (2001). *Helping the helpers not to harm*. NY: Brunner.

Chinnici, R. (1985). Pastoral care following a natural disaster. *Pastoral Psychology*, *33 (4)*, 245-54.

Clinebell, H.J. (1966). *Basic types of pastoral care and counseling*. Nashville, TN: Abingdon.

Corneil, D.W. (1993). *Prevalence of post-traumatic stress disorders in a metropolitan fire department*. Dissertation submitted to the School of Hygiene and Public Health, The Johns Hopkins University, Baltimore.

Dalgeish, T., Joseph, S., Thrasher, S., Tranah, T., & Yule, W. (1996) Crisis support following the Herald of Free Enterprise disaster. *Journal of Traumatic Stress*, 9, 833-845.

Deahl, M., Srinivasan, M., Jones, N., Thomas, J., Neblett, C., & Jolly, A. (2000). Preventing psychological trauma in soldiers: The role of operational stress training and psychological debriefing. *British Journal of Medical Psychology*, *73*, 77-85.

Decker, J. & Stubblebine, J (1972). Crisis intervention and prevention of psychiatric disability: A follow-up. *American Journal of Psychiatry*, 129, 725-729.

Dyregrov, A. (1999). Helpful and hurtful aspects of psychological debriefing groups. *International Journal of Emergency Mental Health, 3,* 175-182.

Everly, G.S. (1989). *A clinical guide to the treatment of the human stress response.* NY: Plenum.

Everly, G.S., Jr. (1999). Emergency mental health: An overview. *International Journal of Emergency Mental Health, 1,* 3-7.

Everly, G.S., Jr. (2000a). Pastoral crisis intervention: Toward a definition. *International Journal of Emergency Mental Health, 2,* 69-71.

Everly, G.S., Jr. (2000b). The role of pastoral crisis intervention in terrorism, violence, and disasters. *International Journal of Emergency Mental Health, 2,* 139-142.

Everly, G.S., Jr., & Flynn, B.W. (2005). Principles and practice of acute psychological first aid after disasters In G.S. Everly, Jr., & C.L. Parker (Eds.), *Mental health aspects of disaster: Public health preparedness and response* (Vol. 1). (pp. 68-76). Baltimore: Johns Hopkins Center for Public Health Preparedness.

Everly, G.S., Jr. & Langlieb, A. (2003). Evolving nature of disaster mental health. *International Journal of Emergency Mental Health, 5,* 113-119.

Everly, G.S. Jr. & Lating, J. (2002) *A clinical guide to the treatment of the human stress response* (2nd Ed.). NY: Kluwer.

Everly, G.S., Jr. & Lating, J.M. (2004). *Personality-guided therapy for posttraumatic stress disorder.* Washington, D.C.: American Psychological Association.

Everly, G.S., Jr. & Mitchell, J.T. (1999). *Critical incident stress management (CISM): A new era and standard of care in crisis intervention.* Ellicott City, MD: Chevron.

Everly, Jr & Parker, C.L. (Eds.) *Mental health aspects of disaster* (pp. 69-78). Baltimore: Johns Hopkins.

Everly, G.S., Jr., Sherman, M.F., Stapleton, A., Barnett, D.J., Hiremath, G.S., & Links, J. (in press). Workplace crisis intervention: A systematic review of effect sizes. *Journal of Workplace Behavioral Health.*

Flannery, R.B. (1990). Social support and psychological trauma: A methodological review. *Journal of Traumatic Stress, 3,* 593- 612.

Flannery, R.B., Jr. (2001). Assaulted Staff Action Program (ASAP): Ten years of empirical support for critical incident stress management (CISM). *International Journal of Emergency Mental Health, 3,* 5-10.

Flannery, Jr., R.B. & Everly, Jr., G.S. (2000). Crisis intervention: A review. *International Journal of Emergency Mental Health, 2,* 117-123.

Flannery, R.B., Jr. & Everly, G.S., Jr. (2004). Critical incident stress management: An updated review. *Aggression and Violent Behavior, 6,* 319-329.

Flannery, R.B., Hanson, M., Penk, W., Flannery, G. & Gallagher, C.(1995). The Assaulted Staff Action Program: An approach to coping with the aftermath of violence in the workplace. In L. Murphy, J. Hurrell, S. Sauter, & G. Keita (Eds.). *Job stress interventions* (pp. 199-212). Washington, DC: APA Press.

Flannery, R.B., Jr., Rego, S., Farley, E., & Walker, A. (in press). Characteristics of staff victims of psychiatric patient assaults: Fifteen year analysis of the Assaulted Staff Action Program (ASAP). *Psychiatric Quarterly.*

Ford, J.D., Ruzek, J, & Niles, B. (1996). Identifying and treating VA medical care patients with undetected sequelae of psychological trauma and post-traumatic stress disorder. *NCP Clinical Quarterly, 6,* 77 - 82.

Frank, J.D. (1974). *Persuasion and healing.* Baltimore: Johns Hopkins University Press.

Galea, S., Ahern, J., Resnick, H., Kilpatrick, D., Bucuvalas, M., Gold, J., & Vlahov, D. (2002). Psychological sequelae of the September 11 terrorist attacks in New York City. *New England Journal of Medicine, 346,* 982-987.

Hunter, R.J. (Ed.; 1990). *Dictionary of pastoral pare and counseling.* Nashville, TN: Abingdon.

Institute of Medicine. (2003). *Preparing for the psychological consequences of terrorism.* Washington, D.C.: National Academy Press.

Johnson, T. (2004). *Finding God in the questions.* Downers Grove, IL: Interfaith

Kaminsky, M.J., McCabe, O.L., Langlieb, A., Everly, G.S., Jr. (2005). Resistance, Resilience, Recovery: A new paradigm in disaster mental health services. In G.S. Everly, Jr & C.L.Parker (Eds.). *Mental health aspects of disaster* (pp. 69-78). Baltimore: Johns Hopkins.

Kaminsky, M.J., McCabe, O.L., Langlieb, A.M., and Everly, G.S. (2006). An evidence informed model of human resistance, resilience, and recovery: The Johns Hopkins' outcome-driven paradigm for disaster mental health services. *Brief Treatment and Crisis Intervention,* On-line Advanced Access, December 7, 2006.

Kaminsky, M.J., McCabe, O.L., Langlieb, A., Everly, G.S., Jr. (in press). An evidence-informed model of human resistance, resilience, & recovery. *Brief Treatment and Crisis Intervention.*

Kardiner, A. & Spiegel, H. (1947). *War, stress, and neurotic illness.* NY: Hoeber.

Kobasa S.C., Maddi, S.R., & Kahn S. (1982). Hardiness and health: A prospective study. *Journal of Personality and Social Psychology, 42,* 168-177.

Koenig, H.G. (2006). *In the wake of disaster: Religious responses to terrorism andcatastrophe.* Philadelphia: Templeton Foundation Press.

Krug, E.G., Kresnow, M., Peddicord, J., Dahlberg, L., Powell, K., Crosby, A. & Annest, J. (1998). Suicide after natural disasters. *New England Journal of Medicine, 338,* 373-378.

Lambert, M. J. (2003). The effectiveness of psychotherapy: What has a century of research taught us about the effects of treatment. Psychotherapeutically Speaking – Updates from the Division of Psychotherapy. Wash., D.C.: American Psychological Association.

Langsley, D., Machotka, P., & Flomenhaft, K. (1971). Avoiding mental health admission: A follow-up. *American Journal of Psychiatry, 127,* 1391-1394.

Larson, D.B., Hohmann, L.G., Kessler, K.G., Meador, J.H., boyd, J.H., & McSherry, E. (1988). The couch and the cloth: The need for linkage. *Hospital and Community Psychiatry, 39*(10), 1064-1069.

Lima, B.R., Pai, S., Santacruz, H., & Lozano, J. (1991). Psychiatric disorders among poor victims following a major disaster: Armero, Columbia. *Journal of Nervous and Mental Disease, 179,* 420-427.

Lindemann, E. (1944). Symptomatology and management of acute grief. *American Journal of Psychiatry, 101,* 141-148.

Lindy, J.D. (1985). The trauma membrane and other clinical concepts derived from psychotherapeutic work with survivors of natural disaster. *Psychiatric Annals, 15,* 153-160.

Litz, B., Gray, M., Bryant, R., & Adler, A. (2002). Early intervention for trauma: Current status and future directions. *Clinical Psychology Science and Practice, 9,* 112-134.

Maslow, A. (1970). *Motivation and personality.* NY: Harper and Row.

Millon, T., Grossman, S., Meagher, D., Millon, C. & Everly, G. (1999). *Personality guided therapy.* NY: Wiley.

Mohr, D.C. (1995). Negative outcome in psychotherapy: A critical review. *Clinical Psychology: Science and Practice, 2,* 1-27.

National Institute of Mental Health (2002). *Mental health and mass violence*. Wash. D.C.: Author.

North, C.S., McCutcheon, V., Spitznagel, E.L., & Smith, E.S. (2002). Three-year follow-up of survivors of a mass shooting episode. *Journal of Urban Health, 79, 383-391*.

North, C.S., Nixon, S., Shariat, S., Malonee, S., McMillen, J.C., Spitznagel, K.P. & Smith, E. (1999). Psychiatric disorders among survivors of the Oklahoma City bombing. *Journal of the American Medical Association, 282*, 755-762.

Nouwen, H.J. (1986). *Lifesigns*. NY: Image.

Parad, H. (1966). The use of time limited crisis intervention in community mental health programming. *Social Service Review, 40*, 275-282.

Parad, L. & Parad, H. (1968). A study of crisis oriented planned short-term treatment: Part II. *Social Casework, 49*, 418-426.

Pennebaker, J.W. (1985). Traumatic experience and psychosomatic disease. *Canadian Psychologist, 26*, 82-95.

Pennebaker, J.W. (1990). *Opening up: The healing power of confiding in others*. NY: Avon.

Pennebaker, J.W. (1999). The effects of traumatic exposure on physical and mental health: The values of writing and talking about upsetting events. *International Journal of Emergency Mental Health, 1*, 9-18.

Pennebaker, J.W. & Beall, S. (1986). Confronting a traumatic event. *Journal of Abnormal Psychology, 95*, 274-281.

Pole, N., Best, S.R., Metzler, T., & Marmar, C.R. (2005). Why are Hispanics at greater risk for PTSD? *Cultural Diversity & Ethnic Minority Psychology, 11, 144-161*.

Rapoport, L. (1965). The state of crisis. Some theoretical considerations. In H. Parad (Ed.) *Crisis intervention: Selected readings* (pp. 22-31). NY: Family Service Association of America.

Richards, D. (2001). A field study of critical incident stress debriefing versus critical incident stress management. *Journal of Mental Health, 10*, 351-362.

Robinson, H., Sigman, M., & Wison, J. (1997). Duty-related stressors and PTSD symptoms in suburban police officers. *Psychological Reports, 81*, 835-845.

Rose, S., Bisson, J., & Wessely, S. (2002). Psychological debriefing for preventing post traumatic stress disorder (PTSD). *The Cochrane Library*, Issue 1. Oxford, UK: Update Software.

Rogers, C. (1951). *Client-centered therapy.* Boston: Houghton Mifflin.

Salmon, T.W. (1919). War neuroses and their lesson. *New York Medical Journal, 109,* 993-994.

Schlenger, W.E., Caddell, J.M., Ebert, L., Jordan, K.B., Rourke, K.M., Wilson, D., et al. (2002). Psychological reactions to terrorist attacks: Findings from the national study of Americans' reactions to September 11. *Journal of the American Medical Association, 288,* 581 - 588.

Shalev, A.Y., & Solomon, Z. (1996). The threat and fear of missile attack: Israelis in the Gulf War. In R.J. Ursano and A.E. Norwood (Eds.), *Emotional aftermath of the Persian Gulf War: Veterans, families, communities, and nations* (pp. 143-160). Washington, DC: American Psychiatric Press, Inc.

Shapiro, D. A. & Shapiro, D. (1982). Meta-analysis of comparative therapy outcome studies. *Psychological Bulletin, 92,* 581-604.

Sinclair, N.D. (1993). *Horrific traumata.* New York: Haworth.

Smith, E.M., North, C.S., McCool, R.E., & Shea, J.M. (1990). Acute post-disaster sychiatric disorders: Identification of persons at risk. *American Journal of Psychiatry, 147* (2), 202-206.

Smith, M.H. (1978). American religious organizations in disaster: A study of congregational response to disaster, *Mass Emergencies, 3,* 133-42.

Smith, M., Glass, G., & Miller, T. (1980). *The benefits of psychotherapy.* Baltimore: Johns Hopkins University Press.

Solomon, Z. & Benbenishty, R. (1986). The role of proximity, immediacy, and expectancy in frontline treatment of combat stress reaction among Israelis in the Lebanon War. *American Journal of Psychiatry, 143,* 613-617.

Solomon, Z., Rami Shklar, R. and Mikulincer, M. (2005). Frontline Treatment of Combat Stress Reaction: A 20-Year Longitudinal Evaluation Study, *American Journal of Psychiatry, 162,* 2309-2314.

Spiegel, D. & Classen, C. (1995). Acute stress disorder. In G.Gabbard (Ed.), *Treatments of psychiatric disorders* (pp.1521-1537). Washington, DC: American Psychiatric Press.

Splika, B., Hood, R.W., Jr., Hunsberger, B., & Gorsuch, R. (2003). *Psychology of religion: An empirical approach.* NY: Guilford.

Stapleton, A., Lating, J.M., Kirkhart, M. & Everly, G.S., Jr. (in press). Medical crisis intervention: A meta-analysis. *Psychiatric Quarterly.*

Stein, B., Elliott, M., Jaycox, L., Collins, R., Berry, S., Klein, D., & Schuster, M. (2004) A longitudinal study of the psychological consequences of the September 11, 2001 terrorist attacks: Reactions, impairment, and help-seeking. *Psychiatry, 67,* 105-117.

Strupp, H., Hadley, S., & Gomes-Schwartz, B. (1977). *Psychotherapy for better or worse*. NY: Aronson.

Swanson, W.C., & Carbon, J.B. (1989). Crisis intervention: Theory and technique. In Task Force Report of the American Psychiatric Association. *Treatments of psychiatric disorders*. Wash. D.C.: APA Press.

Taylor, S. (1983). Adjustment to threatening events. *American Psychologist, 38*, 1161-1173.

Ursano, R.J., Norwood, A.E., Fullerton, C.S., Holloway, H.C., & Hall, M. (2003). Terrorism with weapons of mass destruction: Chemical, biological, nuclear, radiological, and explosive agents. In R.J. Ursano and A.E. Norwood (Eds.), *Trauma and disaster: Responses and management* (pp. 125-154). Washington, DC: American Psychiatric Publishing.

van Emmerick, A., Kamphuis, J., Hulsbosch, A., & Emmelkamp, P. (2002). Single session debriefing after psychological trauma: A meta-analysis. *Lancet, 360*, 766-771.

Verhoff, J., Kulka, R.A., & Couvan, E. (1981). *Mental health in America: Patterns of health seeking from 1957-1976*. New York: Basic Books.

Violanti, J.M. (1996). Police suicide: Risks and relationships. *Frontline Counselor, 4*(6).

Weaver, A.J. (1995). Has there been a failure to prepare and support parish-based clergy in their role as frontline community mental health workers? A review. *Journal of Pastoral Care. 49*, 129-49

Webb, T.E. (2001). Assessing a crisis of Faith and making a pastoral crisis intervention. *International Journal of Emergency Mental Health, 3*, 181-186.

Webb, T.E. (2004). Crisis of faith vs. spiritual cry of distress. *International Journal of Emergency Mental Health, 6*(4), 217-222.

Weiss, D.S., Marmar, C., Metzler, T. & Ronfeldt, H. (1995). Predicting symptomatic distress in emergency services personnel. *Journal of Consulting and Clinical Psychology, 63*, 361 - 368.

Wessely, S., Rose, S., & Bisson, J. (1998). A systematic review of brief psychological interventions (debriefing) for the treatment of immediate trauma related symptoms and the prevention of post traumatic stress disorder (Cochrane Review). *Cochrane Library*, Issue 3, Oxford, UK: Update Software.

Zinnbauer, B.J. & Pargament, K.I. (2005). Religiousness and spirituality. In R.F. Paloutzian & C.L. Park (Eds.) *Handbook of religion and spirituality* (pp. 21-42). NY: Guilford.

Index